The Second

The Second

A Memoir of Love and Commitment

Colleen Burns Durda

The Second: A Memoir of Love and Commitment

Published by CBD Enterprises, LLC, Eden Prairie, Minnesota

A note from the author: The names and identifying characteristics of certain individuals appearing in this work have been changed to obscure their identities and protect their privacy. Conversations, events, and the incidents portrayed in this book are substantially as I recall them. I stand behind these memories.
—CBD

The song "Spirit Voices" is from *The Rhythm of the Saints* album © 1990 by Paul Simon

Library of Congress Control Number: 2021903830
ISBN: 978-1-7366780-0-8 (paperback)
ISBN: 978-1-7366780-1-5 (ebook)

Cover design: Danna Mathias
Interior design: Julie Klein
Author photo: Emily John Photography

For my grandmother:
Evelyn Root Dupont

À vaillant cœur, rien d'impossible.
(For a valiant heart, nothing is impossible.)
—Jacques Cœur

Contents

CHAPTER ONE

The Break

Rage filled my chest as I sat in the cramped exam room, waiting for the ER doctor. Not a garden-variety petulance but an Incredible Hulk–type fury. Posters implored me, in several languages, to report rape, domestic assault, or a lump in my breast. I used them as a call to action. The world had waited long enough for a savior of women, I decided. Voices in my head commanded, "Go. Run." I disobeyed the admitting nurse's order to sit and wait. Grabbing the paperback Bible I'd brought from home, I bolted from the room.

The crowded hospital corridor sizzled with energy on that random Tuesday morning in June 1989. Merging into the human stream, I struggled to shake off the irritation that no media were present to document my first miracles. I made a mental note to hire a publicist as I attempted to pace my steps. I yearned to walk faster, as fast as my racing thoughts, but didn't want to draw attention. Sideshows from me would distract from the real reason for my visit. My inciting anger subsided in a microsecond, replaced by a surge of exhilaration. I was in the flow. These afflicted souls and their healers were my people. I'd waited my whole life for today.

My first thought was to head for the nursery. I craved the sweet innocence of the newly born and who knows, maybe those little angels would recognize my newfound godliness. I scanned the overhead signage for directions, as I had never been inside this hospital. As I looked up, the word ONCOLOGY pulled me in the opposite direction. Yes, that was more like it. I jumped into the elevator as the door opened, intent on starting my ministry curing cancer.

Adrenalin coursed through my body, my heart fluttering as I walked purposefully through the open double doors of the specialty unit. Clutching my Bible, I strode up to a woman reclining peacefully in a vinyl La-Z-Boy. Her long, wavy hair seemed to signify that she was not deep into her treatments. The peaceful smile on her face and tortoiseshell glasses only encouraged me. She wore no makeup, a beige top, and chestnut-brown pants, which contributed to her approachability, for some reason. Large bruises in the crook of her arm and an IV in her hand were my clues she was in chemotherapy.

"Hello, how're you doing today?" I said.

"Oh, okay, I guess," she responded, with a faint upward turn of her lips.

"Do you ever wonder how it's all going to turn out?" I asked her.

"No." The woman smiled. "I know it's going to be fine."

"That's right. You're exactly right. Listen to your doctor. He's a good man." Guessing the gender of her physician made me feel powerful. I touched her arm without the line in it to convey my powers and walked away.

"This healing thing is amazing," I said to myself, eager to try it again.

The next patient I came across was a young girl with her mother. Completely bald, the child wore a pink-and-purple summery outfit, perfectly fitted to her slight four-year-old frame. They were behind a curtain affording scant privacy, and the girl sat on the bed while her mother stood.

In sharp contrast to the woman I had just visited, the mother's dyed blond hair with dark roots, kohl-rimmed eyes, and bright fuchsia lipstick appeared garish, even in the dimmed light. I intuited a lack of trust, distinct fear, and possibly a nicotine craving in the woman. *Wow, I can read minds*, I thought. Despite the blonde's defensive posture, I breached the curtain and tentatively began to speak to the child.

"Is it okay if I talk to your mom for a minute?" Her eyes were sunken into their sockets, and they watched me closely. The little girl nodded.

I stepped to the edge of the bed and asked the mother if she ever worried how the circumstances would turn out.

"No!" she said loudly. "Who are you?" Her face contorted with anger.

I hesitated for a half second, not willing to blow my cover. Then I told her my true identity.

"God," I said simply. With a wave to the child, who waved back, I turned and slipped away quietly. With a quick backward glance, I saw the bleached blonde speaking to another woman and pointing fiercely in my direction. *This can only end badly for me*, I thought. I walked toward the elevator.

"Can I speak to you a minute?" The woman given an earful by the mother gently took my elbow and ushered me to an office marked VOLUNTEER COORDINATOR. Fearless and happy to oblige, at that moment, I felt capable of talking my way out of any trouble I'd gotten into. She showed me a seat and took her place behind the desk.

"Do you have any water? I'm really thirsty," I said. As soon as I spoke, the eerie similarity to the Crucifixion story seemed obvious to me. She didn't make the same connection and looked at me quizzically, then replied, "No." She cleared her throat. "I want to thank you for the work that you do, but you cannot promise a positive outcome." I surmised she'd mistaken me for an overzealous religious visitor.

I glanced at the Bible in my lap, which was actually more of a prop, and felt oddly betrayed. Instant regret came over me for bringing it along. Certain I'd be the star of the sequel, I hefted the book into my arms. Once she decided I understood her message—no promises—she let me go. I had almost made it back to the elevator when we both heard her two-way radio crackle to life.

"We have a twenty-eight-year-old blonde female wearing a yellow tracksuit missing from the ER. Possibly experiencing a psychotic episode." Before I knew it, a different woman appeared.

Her aviator-style glasses, close-cropped hair, and street clothes gave an unmistakable air of authority. With the two uniformed security guards standing sentry, I sensed the jig was up.

"Colleen?" It was more like a statement than a question. "I'm Sunny. You've had a tough morning. I talked to your mom. Will you come with me, please?"

Until that moment, I felt omnipotent, unstoppable, and filled with the Holy Spirit. Now, I was frightened. The modern-day Judas had arrived, and she would lead me away before I even got much of a chance to practice being God.

"I'll go. But you've got to lose the muscle." I tilted my head toward the guards.

"Nope. They stay. Follow me." A large crowd of staff and visitors had heard the radio message and gathered around me. The guards parted the gawkers, and Sunny led me past the public elevator bank to a hidden, private elevator requiring a key. In the far recesses of my brain, I figured this was the end of my life as I'd known it.

When the elevator doors opened, Mom magically appeared, waiting inside. I had no idea how long I'd gone missing or how she had located me. She and I had scurried from my father and my husband when Dad's car pulled up to the hospital. I had ditched her when I abandoned my cubicle in the ER.

There'd been an ominous feeling building in my chest as I not only watched but devoured the news of the past few weeks. "Listen." I spoke directly to Sunny. "Forget everything you've learned as a doctor and hear me out. Today is the day the world changed. Couldn't you feel it coming? Protests in Tiananmen Square, the Ayatollah Khomeini dying—it all meant something big was happening. That *something* was me. Jesus didn't get a chance to finish his work, so God sent a woman to get the job done." Sunny tried to stifle a laugh. I was completely serious.

"I'm not a doctor; I'm a nurse," she said. "We've made arrangements for you to be admitted to Station Forty-Eight."

"What the hell is that? The psych ward?"

I don't remember her response. I tried to run, and the two security guards grabbed me by each arm and lifted me in the air. Suspended above the carpet, I suddenly saw both of my white Keds pressed up onto the wall in protest. The image tripped in my mind. Nothing made sense. I felt kindred to a reluctant dog tugged into the vet. Everything in my power was focused on keeping me from being taken. My life flashed before my eyes, and I saw my future.

With a whimper of defeat, I stopped resisting the guards and allowed them to lead me toward a thick door with a keypad. There went my political career, along with a chance at any career. I was a stay-at-home mom with four little kids, but not even the PTA would have me if they found out I got locked up. Would this follow me the rest of my life? My family would disown me, my friends abandon me, my children not recognize me . . .

"Colleen." My mother's voice broke the litany of loss. I couldn't turn around to face her in my moment of despair. I stared at the locked door. Sunny buzzed the intercom and told them my name. She put a code into the huge metal door, clicked the handle, and the lock opened. I swallowed hard and tried to summon whatever shreds of dignity I had left. Not knowing what was inside, or if I'd ever leave, I submitted and walked into the world of the mentally ill.

Chapter Two

Seeds of Schism

I felt lucky. My sniffles had cleared up enough on that spring morning in 1972 for me to attend a field trip aboard a ferry, the ironically named *Goodtime II*. Our seventh-grade class chugged down the greasy Cuyahoga River, made infamous for catching fire three years earlier. The day loomed gray, and a cold drizzle marred the view of downtown Cleveland. The dreadful weather that day failed to dampen my enthusiasm for my adopted city and my ambitions.

On a subsequent field trip, students interested in health-care careers toured the esteemed Cleveland Clinic. That was where I hatched my plan to become a physician or a researcher and develop a cure for the frequent colds that plagued me as a kid. Living in Cleveland also gave me the Amazonian experience of an all-female high school, which included nuns as instructors. Scholastically, I thrived in the estrogen-charged environment and enjoyed the camaraderie and lack of distractions. When the older girls all wore their hair in curlers to school the day of prom, I eagerly looked forward to when I could join in the fun.

At the end of that school year, in 1975, my family packed up and moved back to our home state of Minnesota, marking the seventh instance I would be the new kid for one reason or another. It became a role I loathed. Introverted and studious, I found making new friends each time a fraught task. The reintroduction of boys into the student mix terrified me.

Sophomore year brought a new school and biology, a favorite subject of mine. The class prankster placed a semidissected frog on my seat as a welcoming gift. Everyone, including the teacher, had a big laugh when I barely missed squishing onto its formaldehyde-laden carcass with my uniform skirt. The boy flashed me a mischievous grin as his way of taking credit for the stunt. While not likely, his fifteen-year-old self may have meant it as an endearment. I seethed silently as my face reddened; I felt like the butt of a cruel joke.

A later chapter tested our knowledge of human anatomy. My 96 percent on the exam skewed the curve for the class. Certainly the one answer I got wrong had to be a trick question: Identify the clitoris? I had never heard of such a thing and couldn't locate it on the blurry, blue-tinged, mimeographed copy. I drew an indistinct line to the nether regions but did not receive credit for my attempt. I wasn't about to ask the male teacher, either.

For our final assignment, we had to write a paper on our career aspirations. Confident of an A, I explained my medical-school goals and threw in a few personal ones. When the teacher tossed my report on my desk, there was a large, red C–. Tearing through the pages, I read his comments. "You must choose whether you want to be a physician or a mother. It is impossible to do both." In that moment, one of my dreams died.

Countless successful people have described tales of being told "No" or "You can't" and how it had invigorated them to prove the naysayers wrong. It didn't work that way for me. The knockout punch landed squarely on my medical career, since I hoped to have four children someday. Four seemed ideal. Far less than the seven I grew up with; nobody would ride by themselves at Disney World, and packages of donuts would divide evenly. It never occurred to me to wish for fewer kids or even question the teacher's edict damning my dream.

I coasted, now rudderless, through the final two years of high school. Feeling a half step behind the rest of the kids, who all seemed to be in established cliques, I spent my time moving from group to group. Prom came and went, both junior and senior years, without an invitation. The most attention I got came from a different male teacher, whose class I didn't take.

He coached some forgettable sport and found teasing me to be quite jolly. If he passed me in the hall, he'd sidle up next to me, forehead so close it almost touched mine. He'd whisper something innocuous in my ear, like, "Do you think it will snow today?" which caused my face to blaze crimson. "Look at her go! Works every time." Then he and his porn-star mustache would continue down the hall, chortling. I learned to hate school after a while. The harassment, witnessed by fellow students, damaged my self-esteem and left me feeling powerless.

When the time came to attend a university, I knew I wanted out and I'd have to forge my own path. Neither of my parents completed postsecondary schooling, and my older sister chose a local community college. The grandest realistic option would be the University of Minnesota's Twin Cities campus.

Despite not knowing where it was located, I got in my dad's car that bright September morning in 1978 to have him drive me to freshman orientation. I watched as we passed the Mississippi from downtown Minneapolis, and the black Chevy Caprice rolled up to the curb outside the student union. I jumped out with my borrowed suitcase in hand. When I turned, Dad had pulled away back into traffic. To an observer, it must've looked like a Mafia roll.

My relationship with my dad at that time was tricky. He refused to allow any disclosure of his income information to apply for a tuition loan. Despite working two jobs, I couldn't manage the costs on my own. This left me completely in the dark as to how I would pay for college. Dad was known to pull off financial sleight-of-hand tricks, so I learned to plow ahead regardless of the uncertainty.

I joined the other students, some of whom were accompanied by both of their parents and suitcases with actual wheels. With a mixture of anxiety and excitement, I surged with the rest of the crowd toward a makeshift stage. A deeply tanned and athletic-looking young man jumped up onto the platform wearing a T-shirt and shorts. His friendly smile and thick, wavy sable hair matched his eyes. He looked astoundingly mature compared to the boys who'd ignored me in high school. His easy manner and a confidence I found incredibly attractive suited his role as the orientation leader.

In a move that stunned me, I pushed my way to the front to ask him a question I already knew the answer to.

"Where do we go next?" I said.

"There are rooms upstairs for small-group breakout sessions," he replied.

I thanked him, completely smitten, and decided college life was going to be fun.

༄ ༄

Later in the day, I noticed a group of girls gathered around some sign-up sheets.

"Oh, you have to come! All the cute guys are going to be there, and I heard you can get a head start on rush," one of them said to her friends. Tired of being left out, I walked up to the papers after the others had moved on. It was for another orientation experience, a weekend camp in northern Minnesota. The handsome senior was listed as a guest speaker on one of the dates. Without hesitation and not having a clue what rush was, I added my name to the list.

That singular decision changed my life. Camp was a series of '70s activities like body painting, trust falls, and an Agape Love feast involving bowls of cut fruit. Most importantly, I realized what it felt like to take risks. I became a joiner. I finagled disco-dance lessons from my former orientation leader by forming a consortium and buying his auctioned services with the currency of the weekend: salted in-the-shell peanuts spray-painted gold.

Freshman Camp introduced me to women and men already in the Greek system, many of whom served as counselors, as well as fellow freshmen interested in joining. The closest I'd been to sororities was watching *Where the Boys Are*, a Connie Francis movie about spring break from 1960. I was shocked to find out the Greek system had been operating for decades at the "U," and some of the girls' mothers, aunts, and sisters had sent recommendation letters in advance to the sororities they'd attended. Knowing no one and with nothing to lose, I gave it my best shot.

I was lucky enough to be placed in the sorority I preferred. On that first day, I looked around at the scores of women. Not simply beautiful, some were title-holding pageant winners. Imposter syndrome tugged at my Sears sweater and whispered, "You'll never cut it here," but I tuned the voice out. My social circle expanded exponentially. I rode the wave of themed, informal exchanges and formal dances. A lot of us borrowed dresses from those with larger wardrobes. The seemingly unending fun buoyed me up over the reality I tried to ignore. I neglected the root reason I was there: to study.

My sleep patterns were disturbed, as I worked late hours at a 24-hour upscale grocery store. I slept through early classes and did a shoddy job of keeping up with my homework. I failed to make the minimum credit/grade requirements because I had to drop a class. This delayed "going active" in the sorority and dumped a big load of shame on me because the whole house knew.

Instead of mending my ways, I turned to my new best friend: denial. Together, we kept up the social end. I stuffed chicken-wire Gophers with tissue paper for the homecoming parade, did dance marathons, and volunteered for whichever committee would have me. I squeaked by with the required grades in winter and was formally initiated into the group. I'd never been so happy.

That spring my dad was diagnosed with cancer. I became completely distracted trying to straddle school, work, sorority, and my younger siblings' needs. I reached my nadir both scholastically and emotionally. The university sent a letter informing me I was on academic probation and in danger of losing it all. Over the summer I worked two jobs and recommitted myself to hit the books when school recommenced.

The following fall, I rallied. I noticed with interest the intriguing senior orientation leader had chosen to stay on for a fifth year and had been elected president of his fraternity. "Hmm," I remarked to myself as he cycled through a series of girlfriends. That winter, a close friend of mine was in charge of a variety show competition between our two houses. It involved a military-themed marching number reminiscent of the film *White Christmas*. Students, paired as couples, were taught simple choreography and wore khakis.

"Okay, Colleen. I know you've had a thing for him for years. I'm giving you JD as your partner for the show," she said.

"The president? Why would you do that?" I answered, thrilled.

"Let's just say you owe me. Big time." She smiled at her handiwork.

JD and I spent practice time getting better acquainted. Aware he was dating someone else, I was nonetheless drawn to his amazing aura. He possessed a tremendous sense of calm and a playful spirit. For my part, I no longer felt like an idealistic freshman agog at the impossibly older upperclassman. Every time our eyes connected, we couldn't help but smile.

We performed our dance number with precision. I barely noticed the rows of other couples on stage. Afterward, once we were in the wings, he lifted me in his arms and gave me an exuberant hug. Two weeks later, the girlfriend had been jettisoned and we were dating.

Suddenly the tumblers in the lock clicked. A world that had been closed to me all my life opened. After a string of random one-off or short-lived dating experiences, I considered someone my boyfriend. This elusive status, part of a couple, had always engendered visions of stability and unending bliss. Instead, I felt scorched by self-scrutiny. *What if he found out I wasn't who he imagined?* My insecurities raged. The overly critical inner monologue I had heard as a single person grew deafening with this precious relationship. JD never said disparaging words to me; I filled the airwaves inside my head all by myself.

I redoubled my efforts in my classes and declared a major of speech/communications. JD graduated in May and started his job search. I finished the summer and settled comfortably into the romance. We didn't talk about the future. In fact, we avoided a lot of topics.

For Labor Day weekend, my parents expected the extended family on Mom's side for a pool party. Forty-five aunts, uncles, and cousins jammed onto our backyard patio. I invited JD. He swam for a short time, then I introduced him to the relatives. He told me he had another party to attend and left soon afterward. On Monday, he called and said the relationship was over. He wanted to move on.

Part of me expected it. The foreboding feeling of inadequacy predicted it wouldn't last. Intense anger also boiled inside me due to the timing. It was humiliating to have him meet my larger family only to have the rug pulled out the next day. I had no inkling what it was like for him. After about ten days of my sulking, Dad finally asked about JD. I told him we weren't together anymore.

"What do you mean? Don't be stupid. He's a great guy," he said.

"Sometimes it's out of my control, Dad," I replied.

"What are you talking about? Did you do something to screw this up?"

My father went on and on until I had to admit, shamefully, I'd been dumped. Dad walked away.

I watched a lot of Ted Koppel on *Nightline* and practically wore the grooves off Carly Simon's *Boys in the Trees* album. Lost and adrift, I imagined going back to school and explaining the absence of JD. With a mixture of bruised ego and desperation, I penned a letter suggesting a reconciliation, and mailed it. In essence, I groveled. JD agreed to meet me at a park near his parents' home. It took a few days of convincing, but we decided to give our relationship another chance. Crisis averted, I could now concentrate on Rush Week, recruiting new members, and going back to school.

JD flew all over the country for job interviews. His résumé

scintillated; his career possibilities were wide open. I didn't want to put any pressure on the relationship. It still felt fragile, and I had two years left of school.

Five weeks later, I found out I was pregnant.

Chapter Three

The Reluctant Bride

Wisps of snow swirled between the few cars in the church parking lot. Pale afternoon light glistened on the icy path as I forged ahead wearing jeans and a ghoulish updo worthy of *The Bride of Frankenstein.* My big day had arrived. Carrying my wedding dress in a bag, I walked toward the circular, contemporary structure with poorly disguised disdain. It wasn't supposed to be like this.

If I ever thought of the place I'd be married, the church would have looked more like Maria's in *The Sound of Music*, only larger. There'd be a long aisle, soaring steeple, and jewel-toned stained glass sprinkling shards of color on my hundreds of guests. My demure smile would reflect a sense of inner calm.

In the nave of my family's church that frigid January day, most of the lights were off. My eyes immediately went to the bright-green burlap banners hung behind the altar. They had nothing to do with a wedding and clashed with the maroon my bridesmaids wore. The dresses, rented and smelling of stale cigarette smoke, reminded me how limited my choices had become. There certainly was no wedding coordinator, so I asked the woman assigned to play the organ if the offensive decorations could be switched out for another color. "It's a little late for that, honey," she shot back and laughed.

My younger sisters, giddy with excitement for their roles in my wedding, twirled around in their floor-length polyester. I clenched my jaw and tried not to lash out at them for being kids. It alarmed me to feel different than everyone else I ran into that afternoon. Truth be told, I felt incredibly conflicted. Without an engagement ring or proposal, I had a hard time believing this was actually happening. Ambivalence clung to me like the layers of shellac holding up my long hair.

JD surprised me as I scurried back toward the bride's room. "Wow! Look at that hair." Irritated at being seen before the wedding and the pall of bad luck it cast, I ran right past him. If our marriage would forever be doomed, I could point to that moment. General embarrassment regarding my coiffure also caused my hasty departure.

Time for the wedding drew near. A tardy guest crept along the far wall. The cavernous church appeared empty, and for a moment I thought there must be some even bigger mistake. This couldn't be my real wedding. One hundred sixty people didn't fill the church like a typical Sunday Mass. As I steadied my father and stepped into the aisle, the organ groaned out a hymn I didn't recall choosing.

His cancer surgeries required a brace in his shoe to lift his foot. I remember how stiff his arm felt as I held onto it. The faces that looked back at Dad and me weren't what I'd imagined at all. Some didn't turn around, others gawked. I'm quite sure I caught a few sneers. My pregnancy, not publicly acknowledged, was a hot topic apparently. If my newly ample bosom wasn't enough of a giveaway, my empire-waist gown looked suspicious. I barely concealed the bump with my small bouquet.

At twelve weeks along, I expanded by the day. My mother had ordered the dress two sizes up from what I'd normally wear, and there wasn't time or money for additional fittings. I'd barely gotten it zipped. Luckily, I was free from any morning sickness, yet an unfortunate case of day rage was a symptom that seemed to come out of nowhere. Extreme irritability at anyone who dared ask me to make yet another decision was all I could muster. Any other mood would have to be faked. With a pasted-on smile, I continued down the aisle.

My father handed me off as best he could. Once he was safely beside my mother, I accepted JD's arm. It was at that moment I wanted to pull the train brake and scream, "Wait! What about my education? My identity? I'm not ready for this. I can't go from 'daughter of' to 'wife of' without even taking a breath!"

But I did.

I repeated vows written by the priest. Writing my own words, like almost every other detail of that evening, had slipped out of my control. The last name I'd known my entire life went *poof.* After we lit our symbolic unity candle from two separate flames, I broke from protocol and accidentally blew out the tiny glimmer of my single self. *Oops*, I thought, *now everyone knows how I feel.*

After the ceremony and dinner, my sorority friends gathered in a circle around me. Sarah, my personal attendant, had ordered a ribbon bouquet as part of a surprise ceremony from the sisters. Their voices blended into a communal sound—a "hum" to find the correct pitch to start their song. I always found this a little corny while we were in school, the whole group-singing thing. Now that I was on my way out, it sounded angelic. They all smiled at me, as if I'd achieved a collective goal. Each sister held one or two ribbons in the house colors. I was the hub of the wheel. When the songs ended, each girl relinquished her ribbon and the streamers dropped to the floor. I stood alone.

In every way I could think of, I no longer felt part of their crowd.

On a night of beginnings, all I focused on were the endings. Four weeks earlier I had taken my last final. After all my difficulties with school, it was painful to have to give it up just when I was getting the hang of it. I had quit my part-time job that I loved rather than answer any more queries about a "bun in the oven." And my father had taken away the last bastion of independence: my twelve-year-old car. I was playing some surreal combination of *Let's Make a Deal* and Mystery Date. I gave up everything I had for the man behind Door #1. It would be revealed at a later time whether I'd chosen wisely to marry my boyfriend, who only recently had had other intentions.

JD seemed much happier that day than I did. Neither of us had much time to contemplate how we were going to approach our new roles, both as marriage partners and as parents. We looked to our own parents' traditional paths and television couples, like Fred and Wilma Flintstone, to chart our course.

To be fair, my idea of marriage was askew. It had originated in romance-novel fantasies, which made the reality a lot harder to take. I assumed JD had an exotic honeymoon planned and wanted it to be a surprise. Along with many other aspects of our life together, we hadn't spoken of it. But instead of jetting away, we spent our wedding night in a local hotel, chosen because they provided a discount coupon with the marriage license application. He went back to work on Monday. The surprise was no honeymoon at all. The wedding embodied both the loss of our former selves and a faith in what was to come. Our child was due in July. We'd soon be a family.

Looking back, the most amazing thing about that time was what never got discussed. JD revealed nothing to his coworkers about his wedding or impending fatherhood. We had no plan for who would write the checks to pay the bills or any concept for what life cost. He went to work at the sales office of a Fortune 500 company every weekday. I stayed home, drank TaB, and watched soap operas. Interrupted dreams, unmet expectations, and fears for the enormous responsibility looming over my belly weren't topics brought up over boxed macaroni and cheese.

Chapter Four

Homemaker in Training

By my calculations, I had six months to transform from a college coed to a domestic goddess. Possessing few skills for this endeavor, I phoned my mother almost daily. Conundrums like "How do you make meat loaf?" or "In what temperature do you wash towels?" vexed me at every turn. JD got into the act by demanding I fold his T-shirts and jeans the "right way" and scolded me when I guessed wrong.

Without money or a lot of options for maternity clothes, I accepted my mother-in-law's offer to teach me to sew. She brought her machine to the apartment two or three times, and together we produced my first creation, a tent-like sundress. I caught on quickly and JD decided I should have my own sewing machine.

Disposable income being scarce, we knew of a salvage store where shoppers could pick through factory seconds, fire-damaged items, and returned goods with missing parts. Sure enough, we found a machine with the serial number etched out and the word KENMORE still legible through the scratches. It had no owner's manual, but the price was right. I didn't know basic functions like how to thread it or what the settings for tension should be, so I decided to call Sears. My ingenious idea backfired when the woman at the store accused me of buying a "hot" machine and hung up without helping me.

Countless knotted threads and mangled seams later, I figured out how to operate it on my own. Cooking and cleaning had their own learning curves, which weren't flattened by my petulant attitude toward housework. Being relegated to all the domestic chores inside our apartment felt wrong and sexist, yet I complied.

Social conditioning taught me to expect that, especially in the absence of a job.

With my patchy success in college coursework, it wasn't as though I'd left a definite career track. The thought of removing one more life stressor that year, by not working, should have been a relief. Instead, I focused on resenting the fact my domesticity descended on me rather than it being freely chosen. Coupled with the reality I was lousy at most of it made my weekdays as a housewife lonely and sad.

Everything changed with the arrival of our baby girl. From the moment of her birth, I felt an innate sense of purpose. My daughter Marni seemed sent from the heavens. Looking into her face, I immediately felt humbled. This old soul seemed sent to deliver me, not the other way around. Going from "me" to "us," even in record time, felt solid and right. So much so, we added siblings to our family in short order.

ꕥ

By 1987, we needed a high-occupancy vehicle. Though the minivan had a bad rap for nerdiness, we bought a new one, and for us, it was the perfect road-trip car. Each child—Marni, almost six; four-year-old Lauren; and our baby, Sophie, fifteen months—had her own version of a car seat. As we headed Up North to rent a lake cabin, I threw in a cassette tape about dinosaurs to pass the time.

While stands of red and jack pines streamed past the passenger window, I had a chance to reflect on how much had evolved for us. JD had changed careers and was working for a developer in commercial real estate. From my vantage point, I'd been promoted twice in six years since becoming a mother. My ability to multitask had improved and now that we lived in our own cozy one-story house, I should have been amazed at what we'd accomplished.

Instead, I felt restless. My sorority friends had finished school, started careers, and were beginning to marry. I could have imagined myself ahead of the pack, but I chose to focus on not having a degree or a paying job. JD worked hard at his job and it consumed him. He also had coworkers and his college friends. The dearth of peers for me in the stay-at-home-mom realm caused the fantasies of working or going back to school to loom large.

I'd been haunted by the specter of Superwoman since my first issue of *Parents* magazine arrived back in the apartment. *Washington Post* journalist Sally Quinn was interviewed and quoted as saying, "I can offer a child so much more at forty than I could as a twenty-year-old." As a twenty-year-old mom, that really didn't sit well with me. I turned the page to see a graphic of a well-heeled woman in a power suit carrying a briefcase and pushing an expensive pram. I guess that should be every woman's ideal. I was so irritated I canceled my subscription. The image never left me, however. It fostered an already brewing feeling of unworthiness. I'm certain when John Lydgate said in the fifteenth century, "Comparisons are odious," he had me in mind.

I looked back at my sleeping cherubs, lulled into dreamland by the fake paleontologist's voice on tape. Hopefully, spending a week with both of their parents present and undistracted would bond us as a family. Turning from the paved road and following the painted signs, we arrived at the resort. The scent of fresh pine needles and the soft breezes off the lake were nostalgic and created new memories all at once. The trek to northern Minnesota had been a tradition for my family growing up. Now I was the one packing the Benadryl, bug spray, and Band-Aids.

JD took over as chief child watcher, and I relaxed by the lakeshore. I spent the week in a bathing suit or my favorite *Miami Vice* T-shirt and pink sweatpants. We prepared meals together, and I felt refreshed by the experience. The week wrapped up and we took our sand-filled Caravan home. Each child chose a miniature box of sugared cereal to munch on for the drive back to the Cities.

JD pulled the minivan into our double garage, and we slipped back into our routine. He unpacked the tailgate area, I brought Sophie in for a diaper change, and the older girls jumped on their bikes and Big Wheels after the three-hour car ride. I had no idea what my future held, but a few concepts were certain: I had a lot to be grateful for, life felt manageable, I had options, and I was firmly and completely in control of my destiny.

Chapter Five

Classic Vinyl

Not long after the rejuvenating road trip, while going about my daily chores and snapping the flat sheet over my bed, I felt an eerie sensation in both breasts. Not pain exactly, more like a thickening or heaviness. Instinctively, I pressed both hands to my chest and squeezed. Granted, a general awareness of my mammary glands had become second nature; each of my three pregnancies had claimed a different set of starburst stretch marks on them. Although it was wildly improbable, a gnawing suspicion sent me scurrying to the drug store for an in-home pregnancy test.

I discovered the test required first-morning urine, so I had to wait until the following day to allay my fears. Waking before JD proved tricky and demanded a locked bathroom door, a rarity in our house. The tests in 1987 were not user-friendly or simple. Following the instructions, I placed the urine I could catch in a small test tube. The results would take a few hours and could be viewed in the slanted mirror fixed beneath the tube and holder. Carefully, I placed the contraption behind a stack of washcloths in the linen closet and returned to bed to feign sleep.

After JD left for the office, the girls and I had breakfast and then went to the park. *No*, I thought. *I have an overactive imagination. It can't happen to me again.* After the shock of my first unplanned pregnancy, I had been desperate for control, so JD and I had carefully calculated and plotted out the conceptions and birth months of both Lauren and Sophie.

I remembered an acquaintance of ours chiding JD at a party. "If you decide to try again, you should spin your sperm at the U. At least then you'd have a chance at a boy." The guy was an ass, but his statement had triggered my thinking. How much control would I expect to exert over the conception of another child? Four kids wasn't out of my realm, and it had actually been part of my plan earlier in life. Choosing the baby's arrival month, at the very least, felt nonnegotiable. I packed up the kids and left the park. It was time to find out my fate.

Locking the door to the hall bath again, I checked the box to determine how to interpret the results. According to the photos, a blob would let me know I was in the clear. If a circle formed, the presence of enough human chorionic gonadotropin would indicate positive for pregnancy. I held my breath and moved the washcloths back. A perfect, dark circle reflected in the mirror.

My heart dropped. The soundtrack of my life felt like the needle got dragged across my favorite vinyl album. Going back to school, finding a job, or seemingly inconsequential stuff like spacing out the birthdays all hit a flash point. None of those events would transpire now. My mouth went dry, and I couldn't breathe.

"Mom, I have to go potty! What is taking you so long?" Lauren wiggled her fingers under the door with a sense of urgency. Throwing the contents into the toilet and cramming the plastic pieces in the wastebasket, I flushed and ran from the bathroom.

My first reaction was to find someone to blame. JD? No, he'd held up his part of our arrangement by providing for us. God? Yes, it was God's fault for allowing this to happen twice in a lifetime. I thought about labor, delivery, and all the physically painful aspects that would happen again. The one person I refused to blame was myself. Badness happened to me. I was a victim of my own fertility. Life took a turn and stepped on me yet again, hard.

I paced the living room and stared at the bare walls. The room, strewn with toys, had never been decorated. I plucked a headless Barbie from between the couch cushions, sat down, and made a promise to myself: everything else about this unplanned pregnancy would transpire on my terms. I could picture my talons digging in, desperate for a sense of dominion.

The idea we were adding to our brood burned a hole in my rib cage, and I couldn't bear the thought alone. I decided to call JD at the office.

"Is this important? I've got a meeting with Dave in ten minutes." Guilt flooded me for bothering him at work.

"I'm pregnant. I took a test this morning."

Braced for the tsunami of shock, I expected cuss words, anger, or something other than what I got. He was completely and eerily calm. JD went into full crisis mode with the absence of panic.

"How can you be sure? How late are you?" he said. I wasn't the only one who knew the drill.

"Forty-two days. My period's not coming, JD. A circle means a baby, and mine was definite. And my boobs are like sandbags."

"Well, at least we've got new insurance at work. We're going to be fine. All six of us. I've really gotta fly. See you tonight."

And with that he appeared to digest this momentous news, slamming the door on feelings or further processing. I wanted to punch something yet felt constrained by his near-instant acceptance. My go-to reaction was to follow my husband's lead. *No mother should feel this way*, I thought. Deliriously happy was the only acceptable reaction to the findings. I boxed up my anger at the situation and started filling the sink with soapy water to wash dishes.

When JD walked in the door after work, he held his arms up in the air to guard his suit jacket from the onslaught of children running to greet him. He wrapped his arms around me. Relieved, I returned the hug.

Marni and Lauren reached a shrill crescendo trying to get our attention. "God, what are we going to do?" I said.

༻ ༺

To keep me focused and moving forward, I had to arrange for a new obstetrician. For a number of reasons, I'd delivered at three different hospitals and didn't have a stellar experience with any of the clinics I'd visited. The variety of experiences helped me formulate my preferences for my last go-around.

The doctor would be male and closer to my age. Female physicians were still rare, and I found it difficult to wedge time into their schedules. My second OB-GYN had been older and made the crack "I wouldn't put you on TV down there" when I asked him if my episiotomy had healed adequately. No one wants to be told that, even if I didn't aspire to that career. I held out hope a younger physician may even be deferential to the awesome power of gestating women.

I wanted to deliver at a specific hospital, located south of us, since it was newish and not likely to be under construction. Trying to labor and deliver with nail guns riveting and poly hanging in sheets, like when Lauren was born, irked me to no end. Armed with my criteria, I pulled a provider directory from the paperwork JD brought home. Starting with the largest group, I picked up the phone.

"Good morning, I need some help in choosing one of your physicians." As I waited for the call to transfer, I wondered if I should just roll the dice instead of practically placing a personal ad to find him.

"I would recommend Dr. Malbec," said the woman after I described my criteria. "He's quite skilled, and his patients think highly of him."

"How old is he?" I felt like I was buying a stallion.

"About forty. Do you want me to put you through to scheduling? There are many other doctors here if you don't click." She sounded exasperated with me, and I hadn't even asked her yet if he was funny.

Oh, what the hell, I finally decided. "Sure."

CHAPTER SIX

Enter the Doctor

Dressed in a maternity jumper embroidered across the bodice, I felt a tad silly. It wasn't my favorite, but it did make me look young. I wanted someone at this new doctor's office to think I was a first-timer wearing this getup. It would make my day.

"Colleen Durda to see . . . ," I said to the receptionist as I searched the staggered rack of appointment cards and found his name on the bottom, "Dr. Albert Malbec." The woman handed me a packet, and I made my way to the last open seat in the room. It was an omen the place was packed, while the decorating left a bit to be desired. The threadbare furniture and dark paneled walls decorated with cheap prints of covered bridges really threw me off. Trying to keep an open mind, I paged through the *Meet the Doctors* pamphlet. On the back cover, I noticed an individual surfing and Dr. Malbec's bio. I thought it was an unusual pose, and I couldn't discern any facial features. The nurse called my name, and I left the booklet on the lumpy sofa.

"Please remain dressed." She handed me a paper dress and a drape. "The doctor will perform the exam after the interview. Dr. Malbec has a student with him today."

"Oh, forget that," I said quickly. "No student for me."

She smiled blandly, like she'd heard that before, and closed the door.

Not long after, the exam-room door opened, and an attractive young man entered. He said hello but didn't introduce himself and wore no name tag. His curly blond hair, deeply tanned skin, and light-green eyes gave off a skater vibe. While his looks intrigued me, I was miffed that my wishes weren't adhered to and decided to play with this student.

"So, is this your first baby?" he said, as he sat down.

"Ha! Yessss!" Vindicated, thrilled this kid took the bait, and feeling a bit cocky, I chirped, "I mean, no, it's my fourth."

Without changing his expression, he made a note in the chart.

"It's okay, I get it. You're not supposed to, but you can look surprised," I instructed.

"I am surprised. I don't have many patients with four kids."

Wait a minute, I thought. *He's too smooth. But if this is Malbec, he's not forty*. Suddenly I felt sheepish and chastened. He asked me a bunch of questions about my health history and deliveries, which I answered dutifully.

"I'll need you to get completely undressed for the exam. I'll be back."

Oh crap, I thought, and kicked my sensible flats under the chair. He was supposed to be less than geriatric and reasonable looking, not young and hot. I whipped my jumper up and over my head and piled my clothes on the chair, careful to stuff my underwear out of view. God had punished me for being too specific, I concluded. I wrapped myself in the paper dress, lifted myself up onto the exam table, and waited with the drape across my lap.

When he returned, he wore a light-blue lab coat embroidered with "A. Malbec, MD" in red stitching over the pocket. He washed his hands and made what sounded like friendly small talk, but my mind drifted elsewhere.

With four pregnancies in seven years, I felt more like a baby factory than a woman. In my career as a mother, I had actually lost count of how many individuals had examined my body with their fingers. Dissociating from my private parts felt natural to me. I sounded like I was tracking and conversing with him, but my responses were mostly an inner monologue as I tried to relax.

He spread the opening of the dress and exposed my chest. Between the chill in the room and his warm hands moving in a circle around each nipple, I didn't have a prayer. I tried to will them limp, but of course that was futile, and my nipples shot forth like dual antennae. Declaring both breasts completely normal, he moved on. Damn, that was embarrassing.

He guided each foot into the stirrups, and I felt my inner thighs tighten with nerves.

"Sorry, this is cold," he said as he applied the lubricant. I kept my eyes focused on the ceiling while I sensed the chilly goop and then his gloved hand enter my vagina. He spoke of his findings as he worked past the ovaries and up to the uterus.

"Cervix is firm and competent. And I'm going to skip the lab test. You are most definitely pregnant. You've got fantastic anatomy for childbirth, by the way. Congratulations. This will go well for you."

At that moment, my mind and body came crashing back together. Not only was he a practiced clinician, but I felt validated. No one, especially a medical professional, had ever congratulated me for achieving a pregnancy. More importantly, I'd never given myself credit, either. My initial mistaken-identity faux pas faded as he snapped off the gloves and reached for my hand to help me sit up. He struck me as kind and considerate.

"Sorry about dismissing the student," I said, not sorry.

He waved off any hard feelings on his part, and his wide smile looked genuine. I stopped at the front desk on the way out to schedule another appointment.

ꕥ

I chose simple black pants and a stylish plaid maternity top to wear to the next appointment. Eager to get on a comfortable level of communication with Dr. Malbec, I chatted with him about the recent World Series championship that had the Minneapolis–Saint Paul area giddy with Twins fever. He asked me to hop up onto the exam table to measure my now obvious baby bump. I stood up from my chair and as I passed him, it felt like his hand brushed my butt.

My cheeks instantly flamed in shock, and I put my palms to my face to cool them. Several thoughts coursed through my mind as I lay on the vinyl wedge covered in white paper. Obviously, that hadn't just happened. What if it was some weird test, like he was checking to see if I would welcome that kind of thing? I never thought about challenging him or asking him if it was intentional. I figured he'd just deny it, and I would look foolish. Instead, I blamed myself for thinking it happened and decided I'd imagined the whole thing.

"Speaking of Twins, you're measuring considerably larger than I'd expect for the dates we're looking at. I'm ordering an ultrasound," he said.

"Don't joke. We're talking four becoming five. There's no way I can deal with that."

"C'mon. We've got it in house. Let's see if our tech is still here and we'll know right away. Do you want to know the sex?" he asked over his shoulder.

"Absolutely not. I'd rather be surprised."

My heart banged around my ribs, and my mouth went dry as I followed him down the hall. Even the suggestion of a multiple birth had me terrified. I buried the thought that he'd flicked my backside as best I could and chose to concentrate on the procedure.

Much to my relief, one healthy baby appeared on the grainy screen. The femur measurement, an accurate indicator of how far along the pregnancy had progressed, put the due date near the end of March. This matched my calculations exactly. My uterus had simply stretched out from its frequent residents.

Aside from feeling like a whale, I had an easy time carrying the baby. In the absence of any concerns or questions, I spent the rest of my checkups chatting with Dr. Malbec about movies, current events, and the high cost of malpractice insurance. On one visit, he asked if I had any questions.

"Yes, but it's not exactly medical. What do you expect your

patients to call you? I've been avoiding calling you anything and it's getting awkward."

He closed the chart and looked me in the eye. "I have lots of friends in my practice. And I would never call you 'Mrs. Durda' because you're younger than me. If I use your first name, I'd expect you should have the same privilege." And so, he was Al to me, and I was instantly part of his fan club. We had a friendly, casual rapport, and I began to look forward to the visits.

One day in January, Lauren came upon me bent over my now enormous belly, as I tried to paint my toenails. "Mama! Why do you need to be fancy? Are you going on a *date* with Dr. Malbec?" Apparently, I had mentioned his name enough times, my four-year-old daughter knew it. She associated nail care and other forms of primping with going out for fun, and the look on her little face told me she was either confused or disgusted. It took the words of a child to tip me off: I was in deeper than I cared to admit.

ꙮ ꙮ

JD and I had fallen into a business-like arrangement. I was "out-go" and he was "in-come," and we knew nothing about meeting in the middle. Naturally, because he was the breadwinner, his work was paramount. Both of us valued his compensated toiling more than everything I did for the family. Subconsciously, I began to resent both my role and my husband. With a minimum of adult attention aimed my way, my conversations with Dr. Malbec took on epic proportions. I spent a lot of time watching Mr. Rogers, but repartee with Al proved much more satisfying.

At an early stage, I had brought my trepidation to JD. I shared with him how strange it felt to have a physician listen to me and laugh at my jokes. He immediately dismissed the notion of Dr. Malbec's relevance and changed the subject. He also predicted the good doctor would soon be forgotten after the baby arrived.

Rather than follow my husband's direction, I took my feelings to my journal. This not only fomented the fantasy but resulted in no objective input. I tried like hell to mitigate the pull I felt toward Dr. Malbec. I sensed, on some level, the relationship was out of the ordinary.

Something about this man made me feel seen. He would comment on my clothing, dresses and tops I'd sewn myself, and tell me I looked nice. It didn't feel strange or intrusive, I told myself; it showed what a nice guy he was. It wasn't a "sex on the exam table" fantasy or lurid type of daydream that I developed concerning my doctor. He appeared to appreciate my intelligence. It was easy to imagine him as someone I would have dated, had fate given me the chance to marry later in life.

He embodied what I wanted for myself. I coveted his confidence, his medical career, and the role he got to play in people's lives. All of his education was focused on the care of women's needs. I decided since he couldn't understand fully what it meant to carry a child or menstruate, he must be incredibly empathetic. By imbuing him with admirable qualities, the reality became unnecessary.

While I thought I was infatuated with him, what I actually fell in love with was an avatar. Not him, only an idealized version of what I wanted him to be. In the pages of my journal, the idea of him grew further and further from reality. Whatever personality traits I may have noticed in my prenatal visits, like a fun sense of humor, keen intellect, and genuine compassion, totally eclipsed the negative ones. On some level I dismissed the arrogance, hints of sexual predation and possible misogyny. I discarded the evidence and those puzzle pieces that didn't support my conclusions of him being a dreamboat doctor.

My attachment to Dr. Malbec made the thought of him being unavailable for the delivery a source of stress. His practice had a policy that each of the docs would be responsible for their own patients' deliveries during the week. On the weekends, they would rotate and be on call every six weeks.

In my thirty-ninth week, I saw Dr. Malbec in his office. I

waited, undressed from the waist down, with a giant paper drape over the lap I could no longer see. He came in, face buried in my chart.

"How've you been?" His tone struck me as concerned rather than curious. He washed his hands, then pulled on some gloves. I held on to the table as he found and began to examine my cervix. Looking away from me, he poked, prodded, and squeezed deep within my body. I winced, and he said, "Sorry."

"You're not dilated or effaced, but according to what you've told me, that could change quickly," he said. I couldn't discern for sure, but this information seemed to put him on edge. I wanted it to be true. I wanted him to see me as special. What I didn't realize at the time, and he admitted later, the aggressive exam was purposeful to put me into labor to suit his timing.

"This weekend I'm on call. When I get the message it's you, I'm going to drop everything and go," he said.

I walked to the parking lot and already felt several contractions before I got to my car. It was Tuesday.

CHAPTER SEVEN

Special Delivery

Thursday night I dreamt of a tropical paradise and an enormous bed floating above a serene blue lagoon. White gossamer linens billowed from the ironwork around the bed, and there was a man in the sheets, his face vague and featureless. Fully dressed, down to his penny loafers, he appeared nonplussed. Unremarkable, except for the cornflower-blue lab coat.

Disoriented by the odd dream, I woke up to the type of strong, rhythmic contractions I recognized all too well. After I gently shook JD awake, we hurried to get the kids going. Stopping every few minutes to breathe through the involuntary tightening of my uterus, I tried to be in the moment. This was the culmination of my career as a child bearer. Never again would I feel these searing pains or the mix of anticipation and exhilaration they brought.

I dialed Malbec.

My desire to speak to him was tempered with anxiety. It would be tragic if my adolescent, smitten feelings became known.

"Colleen?" His voice was soft and soothing, unhurried.

"Hi, uh, my membranes are intact. I lost my plug, and contractions are strong and regular, about eight minutes apart."

He chuckled. I wanted to be a cool, seasoned professional and instead blurted out a status report, *Dragnet*-style.

"Your timing is perfect. I just finished a surgical case. I'll meet you out at the Ridges."

༄ ༄

We dropped the kids off at my parents' house and headed south toward the hospital. I had to breathe through the pains and grip the door handle in the car. JD remained calm and quiet, careful not to turn the car too sharply.

Once we found our way to Labor and Delivery inside the hospital, a nurse named Kathy acclimated me to the room. I got changed into a gown, took a deep breath, and readied myself for my big day. Right after Kathy took my vitals and checked my dilatation and effacement, the phone rang.

"It's Malbec," said a nurse outside my field of view. Her voice sounded scornful, and it surprised me. Kathy stepped out to take the call.

"Your gal is here. She's alert and progressing well. About a four. We put her on a monitor. Membranes are bulging but still intact. What's your ETA? Got it. I'll let her know."

"Your gal" seemed so personal. I wondered whose word choice it was. The nurse stuck her head through the curtain. "He's on his way and will be here very soon." She patted my arm, and I felt like a Holstein.

Ten minutes later, the object of my infatuation stuck his head through the curtain space and walked into my room. He greeted each of the nurses by name, then told me Kathy and he had been classmates in high school. He added his graduation year, and I did the math. I was right, he wasn't nearly forty. I filed it away in my "details I know about Al Malbec" mental folder.

Dr. Malbec asked for a hook to release the amniotic fluid.

"Let's start a flood," he said, reaching in between my legs.

The initial warm rush immediately cooled as the fluid soaked into the pads the nurses laid down. The clear liquid indicated everything was fine, and now the real work would start, I knew.

"Are you a happy camper now?" he said, a satisfied smile on his face. The question seemed odd, so I parried with a gesture of my own. I pushed him playfully in the chest. His muscles felt firm, and his pecs tightened at my touch.

The V-neck of his surgical scrubs revealed dark chest hair, which I'd never seen on him or any man in person. It seemed even noticing it crossed a line. On a day and at a moment I could have focused on my partner, or the task at hand, I chose to concentrate on this doctor I barely knew. The room held a pseudo-intimate ambiance because we all wore hospital garb and the lights were dimmed, although it was morning.

"I'm going to read the paper in the lounge. Call me when she's ready," he said to the nurses, and then he left.

JD stayed with me. He was in khakis and a sweater yet looked oddly out of sorts at my pajama party. He showed no signs of irritation or acknowledgement the doctor had been unusually casual with me. He had more questions about the kids' care but knew better than to ask how I was doing. We had a system. He watched the contractions on the monitor tape, warning me of the coming waves.

"Here's another. Keep breathing. Almost there. Okay, there it goes." Other than when he coached me through the pains, JD and I didn't chat. I surprised myself with how far "in the zone" I went. Distracting myself from the searing sensation by breathing through the contractions, I found I could put my body in a state of not resisting the tightening. I refused any pain meds, and an epidural wasn't offered. I knew what I was there for, remembered the sequence from previous deliveries, and decided if I let my body do its job without fighting the process, it would go faster. Even stronger contractions now gripped my uterus, clamping down as I exhaled in spurts.

The nurses chatted about a Tupperware party. I could hear them behind the curtain. With one last cleansing breath, I tried to sit up in my sweat-soaked bed.

"Get him," I hissed between breaths.

"Yeah, right. What's it been, an hour?" a nurse behind the curtain said.

"I need him. Now," I said.

Kathy appeared. "You need to be checked first, darlin'. I'll wait for a contraction and see how you're doin'." She reached a gloved hand in to measure my cervix. Her eyes bulged. "Page Malbec. She's at ten."

A warming bassinet arrived, and they transformed my bed for delivery. Medical supplies and equipment were moved into the room. He came back and tried to continue the jovial mood, but I stared straight ahead and refused to break my concentration. He immediately responded by taking charge of the room. He requested shoe covers, and my eyes darted to his feet. The black-with-brown, two-tone loafers hardly seemed worth the trouble.

He sat down, his eyes searching for my attention. He said something I didn't understand. He repeated it.

"Colleen," he said for the third time.

Finally, our eyes locked. There was nothing romantic or sexualized about the look, but absolutely everything became blurred except his face.

"This is it," he said. "I understand it's kind of a relief to push. When you feel the contraction, give me one big push."

At that moment, I wanted nothing more than to prove to him how well I could push. Energy mustered up inside me, I pushed from under my ribs through to the circle I imagined was my vaginal opening.

"Now three-quarters of a push," he said.

I took a deep breath, dialed back the ferociousness per his instructions, and pushed again.

This time bones, flesh, and what felt like gallons of warm fluids rumbled out between my legs. I saw the doctor unwind something at least two turns; the umbilical cord had been coiled around my baby's neck. If I'd have given that last push full throttle, I would have choked my baby.

Dr. Malbec picked up the newborn and turned the child faceup.

Time seemed to freeze for a moment as I caught my breath. The gender of this child would be seen by me first.

"It's a boy!" I screamed.

Suddenly, I felt kindred to the women throughout history who birthed male heirs. It was over. My pregnancy and production years finished. Relief, joy, and an exceptional euphoria melded with pain and celebration.

I accepted my new son from the doctor and immediately put the baby to my breast. With all the foot stomping and pouting I had done about this child coming into the world, I wanted him to know he could bond with his mother.

My eyes searched the room for JD. There he stood, apart from and behind the crowd, with a yellow hospital gown thrown over his clothes. His eyes welled over, and he dabbed at them with his sleeve, but he stayed back. I couldn't read his expression and no words came out. I'd never seen JD cry, yet these didn't look like tears of joy. Pain shot through my heart. My chemistry with the doctor must've been obvious to everyone in the room, I thought, especially my husband. Flooded by guilt and deeply conflicted by wanting a different piece of each of these men, I lay back on my pillows and closed my eyes.

With JD in his own world, half the nurses on the baby, and the others monitoring my vitals, I opened my eyes and decided to state what seemed like the obvious in order to lighten the mood.

"I really kicked butt on that delivery." Before anyone could respond, we all witnessed my newborn son turn deep blue.

"We've got a problem," Kathy said urgently. Dr. Malbec grabbed an instrument from a tray near his face. The plastic clamp on the umbilical cord had popped open but within seconds of Malbec's actions stanching the cord, the baby's color pinked up and a second clamp was applied.

"That clamp was defective," he said to the nurses, none of whom responded.

It should have been a moment of supreme happiness, yet I could barely catch my emotional breath. Apparently the doctor was brilliant in his two saves, but had he not secured the clamp properly in the first place? The professionals in the room seemed to leave the question open.

Dr. Malbec repaired a small midline tear. "This might sting a little," he said.

"I can take it," I responded and immediately regretted it.

They took the baby, William, to get his first bath. Shortly afterward, Malbec left for his office, and JD went to work as well. My name and Malbec's appeared together on a whiteboard, pairing us temporarily. I watched as a nurse marked us "DEL" and crossed us out. Kathy wheeled me to my private room.

"Last in, first out," I said, thinking it funny.

"Don't gloat," she responded. When we got to my room she said, "You're in bed one, by the window." Since I'd have the room to myself, I wondered why it mattered. She made no attempt to assist me off the gurney although I was only fifty minutes postpartum. She lowered the rolling cart and watched me walk the ten steps to my bed.

The crisp, white sheets smelled like they'd been boiled in bleach. The blankets felt warm and clean. A different nurse brought in my son, whom I immediately nicknamed Will, wrapped like a cotton burrito. I'd never seen a photo of JD before age three, but I saw his cheeks and nose in my sleeping child.

The events of the morning cascaded over me while I held my newborn. I was certain he could have perished, twice, had circumstances gone differently. Warm, salty tears flowed down my face as I sat there looking out the window. An overwhelming wave of self-pity engulfed me.

Here I was, the self-described queen of labor and delivery, yet I was sitting alone with my baby. Malbec had done his part and left. Why did the nurses seem to have a problem with Al? Their resentment definitely spilled over to me as his patient. And why did JD take off? I looked out my window and watched the clouds outside part as sunshine poured over my wet face. A voice came to me, ancient and familiar, yet I'd never had an experience like it before.

"I saw how you delivered your baby. You did a fantastic job.

I'm proud of you. Take care of him and all of your children. I am with you always." The voice spoke through the rays of sunshine, more felt than heard.

It was one final piece I didn't question or mention to anyone. I simply cried. Little did I realize, it was the beginning.

ꟷ ꟷ

The next day I walked down to the nursery to visit the pediatrician.

"I can do the circumcision now, if that's okay?" she said.

"No, thanks. I want my OB to do it. I discussed it earlier with Dr. Malbec, and that was the plan."

She seemed put out, but I ignored her irritation. We discussed home care for the soon-to-be-circumcised Will, since I considered myself a professional at the general aspects of newborn care. The pediatrician turned to leave, and a man approached the nursery.

"Oh my God, it was you!" I ascertained he was a new dad. "I'd recognize your voice anywhere. The whole hospital heard you say, 'It's a boy!'"

I laughed, which hurt my tender midsection. I explained he was the eighth grandchild on JD's side and first boy. Accepting congratulations from everyone in the now full room of people, I excused myself and headed back to my room.

Settling back onto my bed, careful to keep the blue Chux pad under me, I recalled the delivery. Just as I remembered something Dr. Malbec had done, he walked in.

I felt my face turn bright red. *Oh great, now he knows I was thinking about him.* Even though this was impossible, I still felt self-conscious.

"I have a surgery scheduled for tomorrow, so my partner will be discharging you. How are you feeling?"

I have no recollection of the rest of that conversation. I thought he'd be there because it was "his" weekend. Hearing I wouldn't see him again the next day crushed me deeply. It wasn't a proportional response. Devastated, and confused by my reaction, I blamed my fluctuating hormones.

Chapter Eight

Make a Move

The supposed ultimate in motherly goals achieved, I returned home to complete chaos. I had three beautiful daughters, and the arrival of the male child should have secured my position as content. Instead, I felt lost.

Days blended into nights. The baby nursed on demand, laundry piled up, books needed to be read, food prepared, and Marni's kindergarten bus met twice a day. Had I known what to call it, I was definitely experiencing postpartum depression. I dismissed the sadness as temporary. All I needed was more sleep and a schedule I could keep. But something else gnawed at me as I dragged myself from chore to chore. I missed the weekly visits with Dr. Malbec. Imagining we were friends provided an escape from the grueling demands of my young family. Shoving guilt and shame into the far corners of my mind, I sought relief and a diversion from reality. I figured the only remedy was more Malbec.

I concentrated on losing weight. I wanted to wear my favorite dress to go back and visit him for my six-week postnatal checkup. The dress was tea length, polished cotton, with tiny pastel flowers. It had peekaboo openings between the buttons up the back. I found a backless bra at a specialty store to wear so the back clasps wouldn't show through. The bra straps crossed near my waist; it was clunky looking but served a purpose. Fingers and toes were polished, hair highlighted, and my spirits prepared more for a clandestine rendezvous than a visit to the doctor.

I walked into the lobby feeling confident and deliriously happy to be alone with Dr. Malbec for a few minutes. I checked in and sat down across from a middle-aged woman. Tossing aside a

Redbook, I noticed a copy of *Sports Illustrated.* I needed a distraction to calm my nerves and casually thumbed through the magazine. A centerfold of José Canseco in his Oakland Athletics uniform caught my eye.

I felt my nipples reflexively tighten and heard a splashing noise on the page. My overactive breasts became confused, and milk began dripping from my beautiful dress. In my haste to look fabulous for Dr. Malbec, I'd forgotten to wear any shields in my fancy bra. The woman across from me squirmed in her seat but said nothing. Having a spectator to my lactation debacle made my humiliation worse.

"Colleen?" the nurse called.

I grabbed the magazine, pressed it to my chest, and walked into the clinic area.

She put me in a room and told me to leave my bra on and change into the paper gown and drape. I smiled weakly and let her leave. There was no way Malbec was going to see this contraption of a brassiere or how wet it was. Despite my rookie mistake, I knew enough about leaky breasts after four kids to know exposing them to the open air was more likely to stanch the milk flow. So that's what I did.

Soaking my lovely dress, even though he wouldn't see it, shook me up. I felt vulnerable and foolish. I blamed myself yet again and decided I deserved the humiliation for putting forth so much effort toward this virtual stranger.

He walked in and washed his hands. He looked painfully handsome with his tanned skin and dark-blond curls. I wanted to cry.

"How have you been, kiddo?" he said. The crinkles at the edges of his eyes made him appear younger, or at least that's what I imagined. His smile disarmed my anxiety about the dress.

"I was fine until I ruined your magazine. I'll be taking that one home."

He seemed to shrug it off. "Speaking of home, how are things?" he said.

He's probably not asking how my carpet is holding up, I thought to myself. I felt transparent, like he knew there was trouble in paradise, yet I wasn't ready to open up to him. I hadn't yet admitted any overt dissension between JD and me to myself.

After he examined me, the conversation turned to resuming my sex life. What I couldn't articulate were the psychological barriers to intercourse after a vaginal delivery and episiotomy. All I could come up with was something about fear of pain.

"Oh, you're not tight at all," he said, thinking he'd allayed my apprehension.

Right there, I could have walked out on him over such a ridiculous remark. Instead, denial kicked in again and I erased the idiotic comment from my memory of the encounter. It wasn't a rubber band he'd referred to, and the careless way he referenced my body demanded more of a reaction. I was so desperate to maintain my pseudo connection to him that I tolerated his complete insensitivity.

He reached for my hand to help me sit up. I really wasn't looking forward to putting on my cold, milk-soaked clothes. We said our goodbyes and as I drove home, I inexplicably began plotting how and when to get back there.

ꕥ

JD drove the six of us around in our minivan the following Saturday. The two older girls sat buckled into the first back row in booster seats. Sophie reclined in her car seat in the second row, and I rested in the third, nursing my newborn next to his car seat. I looked out my slightly tinted window at the traffic on I-494. I saw a young man in cool sunglasses, driving a sports car and wearing scrubs. My heart ached.

I missed my own doctor and the relationship I imagined we had. With this baby, the doctor had also assumed a different set of roles. "Advisor," "friend," "conversation foil," and some sort of "adult playmate" seemed to describe our relationship. The dynamic had grown casual between us and the professional boundaries blurred.

Now, with him gone, it forced me to confront inadequacies in my life. I craved friendship. JD and I shared tasks but no real feelings, positive or negative. This created a vacuum, and Al had walked right into it. Postpartum depression seeped into my soul again. Instead of acknowledging the pain directly in front of me, I went with my go-to remedy: start another project.

With the delivery still fresh in my mind and my body in the process of recovering, JD drove the family that day to look at a suitable neighborhood to relocate our brood. An acquaintance of JD's from work told us about a model home available in a new development, in an up-and-coming suburb.

Eden Prairie held the promise of youth. We went driving hoping to find swing sets, bikes, and strollers. It could be the best of both worlds: a newly constructed house and one we could move into quickly.

The house looked welcoming from the outside: a two-story with an attached double garage and light-gray painted cedar with white accents. A brand-new elementary school, situated directly behind the house and separated by an idyllic pond, had opened the year before. Down the street two blocks, a library and shopping mall waited for us. We made an appointment to see the house the next day.

Stripped of its showcase furniture, with sun-faded wallpaper and window treatments, the former model didn't show well. We passed peach and green walls and a tiny family room, then made our way upstairs. Elegant French doors caught my eye.

"What's in there?" I said.

The realtor gave me a showman's smile, took both knobs of the doors, and swung them open. An owner's bathroom the size of another bedroom took my breath away. Fully carpeted, it held a huge Jacuzzi tub, his and hers separate showers, and two sinks, each with their own vanity.

"Sold," I said.

࿇

I had to prepare my cramped little house for strangers to traipse through, which meant cleaning every closet and the kids' rooms, with no place to hide any messes. Nursing a baby, trying to keep a toddler occupied, and finishing up the school year for Marni and preschool for Lauren left me nearly wiped out. After three weeks of frantic scrubbing and packing, we put the house on the market. Mercifully, it sold in six days. I pushed myself to a level of near exhaustion, saying, "When I get that beautiful new house ________." (I'll forget about the doctor, my marriage will be healed, I won't snap at my kids, etc.)

We finally moved out the second week in July, on what had to be the hottest day of the year. The doors were open all day, yet the air was still and humid. I grabbed the sheets off Marni's bed, balled them up, and threw them into an unmarked black trash bag. The rest of the move went fairly well but by the end of the day, the kids were cranky.

We put together Will's crib and beds for the girls in their new rooms. I couldn't locate the black bag containing Marni's sheets, so she slept in a sleeping bag on her mattress. Sophie hadn't napped all day and screamed, beside herself, and it only got worse when her beloved blanket went missing. She wailed fiercely and kept the whole house awake. In some misguided fit of maternal problem-solving, I decided we must have left the blanket at the house we no longer owned.

At two a.m., I drove to my former house, stuck a spare key we hadn't surrendered in the door, and walked in. I hadn't prepared what to tell the new owners if I encountered them. They had told us at the closing they wouldn't be moving in right away, but this was an unconscionable risk. My toddler's shrieks still echoed in my ears. Wild-eyed, I walked through their house. I noticed used champagne flutes on the counter, and I panicked, worried I'd find them in flagrante in their own house. I ran through each empty room but found nothing, especially the blanket. I relocked the door and drove back to the new house.

Sophie had fallen asleep but still shook when she inhaled, having cried for so many hours. The next morning, I found and opened what appeared to be the last nondescript plastic garbage bag of the move. There, inside her older sister's ball of Rainbow Brite sheets, was the prized blanket. Nightmares about sneaking into that other house, and this time getting caught, haunted me for years.

Since we couldn't afford the thousands of dollars the builder wanted for the useless, sun-bleached window treatments, they had removed the draperies before we moved in, resulting in a fishbowl effect. We had stretched to afford the house and didn't have the cash for blinds on all those windows, either. We put sheets up in our bedroom, but the other rooms were creepily open. The feeling of being watched by passing cars, I firmly believe, contributed to my difficulties the following year.

The neighborhood itself, forty-three homes and over seventy children, proved ideal. The parents in the other homes were slightly older than JD and I, making them perfect candidates for friends. With no more visits to Malbec on the horizon and this huge financial and emotional investment, I felt poised for new beginnings.

CHAPTER NINE

Cutting Edge

"Colleen, you know the Church's standing on artificial birth control," my mother scolded, on a roll. "And another thing, now you're inventing problems to get back in to see that doctor. I don't like it." She wrapped the string around her tea bag and squeezed it against the spoon. The Earl Grey helped warm us against the slight autumn chill. My mother's uncharacteristic challenge surprised me, but I considered it a fair price to pay for all the babysitting she did.

"Mom, JD and I traveled to that parish out in Timbuktu to learn natural family planning when I was eight months pregnant. That was completely humiliating. I decided I would never again allow the Church into my bedroom after that fiasco."

My mother cleared her throat. She and I never had the teen sex talk and by the time she mentioned anything, I found myself already with child. It took many years before I understood how profoundly my lack of sex education affected me. That blind spot had created havoc in my life. Taking control of my fertility meant deciding my destiny. She had me dead to rights on the doctor, though, but I couldn't admit that to her.

"I know you're not a big fan of Dr. Malbec, but he is my resource for birth control." I tried to sound definitive. We sipped our tea in silence. My mother had a way of leaving me feeling involuntarily transparent.

ꟷ

I locked our bedroom door after we had bathed, read to, and tucked in the kids. JD flopped down onto our bed and flicked the remote at the television. I walked up and shut it off.

"What's the deal?" he said.

"We need to talk about what we're going to do. Are you completely certain we're finished having kids?" I said.

"Absolutely done," he replied.

"Okay, me too. Who's going to have the surgery?" A foregone conclusion for me, framing it up to him needed a deft hand.

"Maybe we should both do it," he said.

"Good idea, but total overkill. I see it like this: I've got to stop one egg a month. You're talking, what, millions of sperm? I like my odds better," I responded.

"You've been through enough. I'll get snipped, sit on an ice bag for a weekend, and take care of it."

His willingness surprised me, although it shouldn't have.

"I'm the one whose body pays the consequences if there's a fail. Besides, I have a relationship with a doctor already. We don't know any urologists, but maybe I'll ask him for a referral." I held my breath.

"Yeah, you're right, Colleen. Dr. What's His Name should take care of it." JD rolled onto his stomach and turned on *L.A. Law*. Mission accomplished. Decision made.

༄ ༄

In the absence of a professional therapist and unable to process my conflicted emotions about my identity, marriage, and fantasy life, I took lots of baths. While in the tub, I journaled about Al Malbec.

Pouring out my feelings to the page served my own interests. The imaginary relationship legitimized in the privacy of my mind, and the fantasy drove a wedge into my marriage. Needing both short-term and permanent birth control, I convinced myself to call Malbec's office and made an appointment for a consult.

The nurse sat me in an exam room, and I waited, pretending to read a magazine. After she closed the door, I stood up to examine the 3D model of female reproductive organs perched on the counter. I had the ovary-fallopian-uterus relationship mastered in tenth grade. What piqued my curiosity? The existence of the elusive clitoris. Ever since my biology final where I had failed to identify the sex organ, I'd assumed it was mythical. Someday I'd ask about my lack of orgasm, but today I had other items on my agenda. At the ripe old age of twenty-eight, I needed a primer on conception avoidance until the surgery.

With a quick double knock he swept into the room. His hair cut shorter now, it showed signs of thinning near the top. He narrowed his eyes and extended his hand while posing his trademark question, "What's up?"

My jaw tightened and easy, breezy smile froze despite an attempt to play it cool. I could've handled the subject easier without the schoolgirl crush, yet the harder I tried to suppress my feelings, the more nerve-racked I appeared. I sputtered something about wanting a tubal ligation and some kind of birth control for the interim.

He rolled his eyes and exhaled slowly, obviously relieved. It dawned on me my cryptic request for a "consult" could have been code for a myriad of unfortunate symptoms women bring to their doctors. He scribbled something on my chart. Someone knocked on the door, and he excused himself to take a call. I peeked at his note: "Sterilization Consult-Patient is anxiety ridden." What? How dare he write me up like that? I took time to reset his impression of me before he returned.

When he sat back down, I told him I'd looked into it and my insurance would only cover the tubal surgery if deemed medically necessary.

"Bullshit," he said immediately. "Pardon my French, but that's ridiculous." He threw his pen on the desk. "You are officially hypertensive."

"My blood pressure is fine," I explained, not picking up his drift.

"Hypertensive patients can't take the pill. They'd need an alternative, like surgery."

I blushed, feeling slow on the draw. His intellect impressed me, and he was obviously willing to help me. "How many of these have you done?" I said.

"About a thousand." He shifted on his stool, lacing his fingers over one knee. "Now I have a question for you," he said.

"Shoot," I replied.

"How's your marriage?" He stared at me impassively. The question seemed loaded every which way to Sunday.

"I'm not trying to get into your business. I've never had to reverse one of my own, and I don't want you doing this out of spite."

He didn't understand the dynamic of my relationship or probably care. It should have dawned on me then his paramount concern involved his perfect scorecard as a surgeon rather than the trajectory of my life. I might have easily scheduled something then; it would have given me a reason to call him back. Instead, I presented it to Malbec as if JD and I were still unsure who would have the surgery and asked him for a urologist referral. My moment of indecision proved I just wanted more contact with my doctor. Damn my mother for being right.

"Okay, now I need contraception for the time being. What have you got that's nonhormonal, noninvasive, nonabortifacient, and one hundred percent effective?"

Nodding, he had an idea. He told me to get undressed from the waist down and he would be back shortly.

He returned with sizing rings for a diaphragm. Describing how the actual device would fit over my cervix and behind my pubic bone, he asked me to practice with the circle. His word choice was odd, however.

"I need you to be comfortable with this and not leave it in your nightstand. I want you to play." He left the room. A dissonant chord sounded in my head. Instead of listening to it or even acknowledging his strange comment, I did as he instructed, moving the ring in and around. It felt clinical and numb.

"Did you enjoy yourself?" he said, as he returned to wash his hands.

"Not really," I said.

He laughed, seemingly at me and his own ribald joke. "Go ahead and get dressed. I'll get you a real one."

This time, he didn't knock, and he caught me literally with my pants down. Ignoring the impropriety, he walked up and stood very close to me. I had to turn away to zip my jeans. A nervous giggle bubbled up as I tried to tamp down the reprimand he deserved. I was not in control of my reactions or the situation. He held an empty box and wore the rubber circle on top of his hair.

"When you don't need it anymore you can use it as a hat. Or maybe a tambourine," he said as he tossed it to me. He wrote the name of a urologist on a prescription pad. He started to hand me the slip, then playfully pulled it back. "You're perfect. Everything is perfect. Call me if your husband backs out on you." The last sentence hung in the air, poised between proper and clearly not. We brushed shoulders as we left the room together. "I know you're going to call," he said with a smile.

Something akin to seductiveness continued to lure me in as I ruminated on his words for weeks. Despite my deep-seated feelings of insecurity, I felt chosen by Dr. Malbec. The invisible, unspoken barrier I'd always sensed between any physician and me eroded into vapor.

ℌ ℭ

My marriage suffered a deep freeze. I felt pulled into the vortex that was Malbec and shut down by my husband's refusal to discuss my feelings about the doctor. JD acknowledged our communication difficulties and agreed to try a new therapist. The first one we had contacted about five months earlier had flamed out after the one hour. She assessed us to be in crisis, and JD declared her a "quack." We dropped the subject of outside help and didn't return to her. I declined to share our problems with any of my family or friends, which only increased the pressure I experienced. I didn't feel listened to in my marriage. I was hurting, and JD wanted to plow past the problems by ignoring them and hoping they'd dissipate with time. The next available opening to see the new psychologist was weeks away, but I grabbed it.

Grappling with a troubled relationship caused me to reach out to my mostly imaginary friend, Al. Of course, I had to schedule the surgery, legitimizing the reason for contact. I left a message at his office and then stared at my phone. I imagined telling him my marriage troubles and his caring, sensitive response. The kitchen phone jangled on its cradle, causing me to jump.

"Colleen? Al Malbec returning your call. How are you?"

"I'm ready for the tubal," I blurted, careening past any further personal revelations. Wincing at my obvious nerves, I heard him laugh.

We confirmed a week that worked for both of us, which was in February. He told me his nurse would set up the specifics. The conversation ended in less than three minutes.

"Thanks, dear," he whispered as he hung up.

Oh, don't do that. Don't sound sweet and lovey-dovey. I'm already messed up over you and your blurred boundaries. I loved and hated those interactions. Too brief, yet I managed to feel self-conscious, juvenile, and off balance at their conclusion.

Malbec's nurse had scheduled a pre-op physical for the Friday before the procedure. I decided to take my now eleven-month-old son, thinking the baby would give me a distraction from feeling nervous. Eschewing any fancy outfit, I wore jeans and a multipastel cable-knit sweater. I stood in the anteroom of the clinic, got weighed, and looked over to see Dr. Malbec changing into a sweater. My first thought percolated an unlikely reason for the wardrobe switch. He wanted to be extra casual for my appointment. He must've seen what I wore. I chastised my running monologue for overthinking, grabbed the baby from the nurse, and went into an exam room.

The nurse instructed me to remove my sweater and leave my bra on. He'd need to hear my heart and lungs. She did not provide a gown. Al knocked and entered; the nurse slipped out. He greeted both Will and me, putting me instantly at ease. I set my son on a blanket on the carpeted floor, with a few toys, and then sat on the exam table.

Al put his left hand on my bare back and moved the stethoscope with his right. He listened through my chest, then moved to my back, never moving his left hand.

"Have you been one thousand percent careful with contraception?" he said finally.

As he spoke, I felt his hand caress my back, rubbing up and down.

Okay, that's not weird, I tried to convince myself. *He's just being supportive.*

"It's not exactly an issue. We're seeing a counselor," I replied. The first statement was a bald-faced lie; the second a simple, almost irrelevant fact.

"What if Mr. Goodbar comes along and says, 'I want lots of little babies'?" The back rub continued. "You're young enough and good-looking enough. You have no idea what your future holds," he said.

It remained unclear if he was referencing himself wanting children or all the potential suitors I'd have if my marriage were to disintegrate. Either way, my head started swimming. Forget fight or flight; I froze.

I looked down and pretended to laugh him off, lightly bumping the arm rubbing my back. He didn't move it until his pager went off. "Get dressed," he said. "I'll be right back."

When he returned, he put his hands on my shoulders, near my neck. Without prodding, he launched into a story about how his first marriage had fizzled and how counseling didn't always fix relationships. I had no clue what my surgery had to do with his life, yet he seemed to take my decision personally.

"Do you have any children?" I asked him, finally.

"No, but there's one on the way." His eyes bore into me, as if to drive home his message. "You see, circumstances happen you don't expect." My overthinking brain went into overdrive. *Is he surprised about his child? Is he insinuating I have more babies in my future? What, exactly, is his point?* If a camera crew were to jump out at me just then, it would have made more sense. Smile, you're not in a real doctor's office. You're on *Candid Camera.* I picked Will up off the floor.

"I'll be here for your annuals for thirty years. I'm not trying to deliver your next fifteen kids. I'll do the surgery if you're ready." He took my arm and held me and my baby close. Al lifted my baby's bag onto my shoulder and rubbed the back of my neck.

"Listen, you have five days to call me and cancel this. If I don't hear from you, we're on for Wednesday."

If I stopped and asked why he said half the remarks he did, or even if half of the inferred meanings were true, I feared he would turn them on me and claim he was misrepresented. The worst I feared: it was all in my head. It never dawned on me to quit him and find a new physician. At this point, I still craved the type of pseudo-intimate attention he gave me.

In a daze, I made my way to the minivan and strapped the baby into his car seat. Like everything else that should have been questioned, stopped, or even acknowledged, I did nothing. By the end of the evening, home with my family, I'd convinced myself I'd imagined his comments and back rubs.

∞ ∞

I walked in for my surgery a week later, hopped up on the table, and settled myself. My glasses were left in a locker with my lemon-yellow tracksuit and lacy undergarments. The gown, tied tightly to close the gaps, fit poorly. The anesthesiologist spoke to me, but I zoned him out, eager to locate my surgeon among the masked faces peering at me.

"Go ahead for Dr. Malbec," the speaker echoed into the OR and I tensed on the operating table. Two minutes later, I sensed the energy in the room quicken, and I felt his arrival. A figure leaned down inches from my face. I could see the familiar crinkly smile lines and green eyes behind the mask.

"Good morning," I said.

"You didn't change your mind?" Al lifted his head to look around, then bent close to me again. "I can tell all of these people to go away if you want me to." He kept his face an intimate distance from mine as if the rest of the medical personnel weren't watching.

"I'm ready," I said.

Dr. Malbec reached out his gloved finger to rub my exposed collarbone. Then he stood up straight and formally acknowledged the team for the first time. The nurse anesthetist's soothing voice asked me to count down from one hundred by sevens. I got to ninety-three and lost consciousness.

My next thought was, *What are those clanging noises?* I heard people retching. Emesis basins were the source of the metallic sounds. I peeked beneath the blue fabric to see sutures near my naval. No turning back now.

JD opened the curtain. "You're awake? What the hell is wrong with this place? I've been sitting in the waiting room for two and a half hours. Not once did anybody tell me what was going on."

"I'm sorry, JD. There must be some explanation," I said.

"Yeah, your precious Dr. Malbec is an asshole," he said. "He should have come out to find me and let me know you were okay."

"You're stressing me out. Please stop yelling," I said.

He fumed in silence all the way home from the hospital.

I slept off the effects of the anesthesia for the rest of the day in my own bed. My mother had disagreed with my decision yet was kind enough to come over and help with the kids. Resting gave me time to gather my thoughts. It was actually fortuitous I had feelings for my doctor, I decided. It allowed me to imagine under what circumstances I'd want to have another baby. What if Al Malbec, or an equivalent, wanted to marry me and have more children? Too bad, came my response. I have real children, four of them. I fantasized about romantic getaways, but my babies were actual, not hypothetical. My marriage may have been on the ropes, but my children were here to stay.

The next day, we had the marriage therapy appointment. The phone rang while we were getting ready to leave, and my mother said it was Malbec's office. I quickly returned the call. His wife had their baby, and he'd be taking time off. They needed to schedule me with a nurse practitioner to remove the sutures. The information rattled me. My fantasy and reality collided, causing a rift in my psyche. Just the news he'd be taking a leave when his child arrived reminded me of how quickly JD had returned to work each time I gave birth. My heart ached.

My eyes went to the wrapped gift in my closet, a white onesie I'd purchased to give to him. I'd signed the card, FROM YOUR 1001ST TUBAL SURGERY. What a fool I'd been. We weren't friends. We were nothing.

In her office, the therapist listened intently as we described some of the problems my husband and I had been experiencing and the history of our relationship. She asked if either of us had something to add separately. JD stepped out and I told her I was angry, frustrated, and emotionally attached to someone else.

"Does your husband know?"

"He thinks it's a joke." I felt the words fall out of me like nuts and bolts from a broken machine. I'd held it in for so long, and admitting my feelings to a professional reduced me to a pile of emotional rubble.

"What about the doctor?"

"We've never directly discussed my feelings for him. I feel close to him, and I'm not convinced I'm alone in that."

"So, it's a fantasy."

The word stung. She dismissed everything to do with my intuition as unfounded. Stripped of what had sustained me for months, I wanted to run screaming from the room.

"I'll tell you something else. If I find out it's anything more than that, I'll report him."

Instinctively, I went to protect Al. Whatever he was, we had a bond between us that meant more to me than almost anything. I decided right then, it wasn't safe to share truthfully with this woman. She called JD back into the room. "Maybe you should come in by yourself and put the marriage counseling on hold for a bit," she said, looking at me. JD, more than happy to avoid the conflict and have someone other than him listen to the doctor saga, appeared visibly relieved. Confused and desperate, I agreed to the new arrangement. She'd only get as much as I felt like telling her.

ꕤ

Going back to Malbec's office knowing he wasn't there felt empty and sad. I brought the gift in a small bag, not knowing what else to do with it. The nurse called me in.

"Wow, he really bruised you," she said, snipping the threads near my naval. I didn't reply. Then she looked at my chart. "You have four kids? What are they? Four, three, two and one?" Her question insulted me. This clueless woman was a poor substitute for the man I needed, and I didn't care for her insinuations.

"I've got a gift for Dr. Malbec. Can you make sure he gets it?"

She took the box wrapped in pastel footprints and gave me a quizzical smile. "I'll put it in his box. That's awfully kind of you. People usually don't buy presents for the dad."

I left her staring at me. Passing a wastebasket, I crumpled the empty Dayton's bag and dumped it in the trash on my way out the door.

CHAPTER TEN

Close Encounters

Feeling alone and shameful about my continued fixation, I desperately needed friends. In the winter of 1989, I joined a playgroup in the neighborhood, ostensibly for the children. We took turns, rotating the hosting duties every Monday, and each of the half dozen moms had a two-year-old. Sophie enjoyed the playmates, and the chance to catch up with the women eased my loneliness. In the course of chatting, invariably the topics of pediatricians and gynos came up. I casually mentioned the name of my OB-GYN and carefully self-censored to keep the personal details about him quiet.

One week, a woman named Donna approached me.

"Didn't you say you saw Al Malbec?" she asked.

"Yeah, why?"

"We were at a fortieth birthday party last weekend, and he was there." She sipped her coffee, completely unaware Klaxons sounded in my head at the mention of his name.

"I guess his wife was in the same sorority as my sister-in-law," she said, righting an upended toddler.

Please don't say it's mine, I silently prayed. She mentioned the house. I thanked God it wasn't the same one. Tempted to pump her for more information, I fought the urge.

"We went bowling, if you can believe that. He mostly hung around the snacks. I don't think he knew a lot of the people there," she said. I smiled and attempted to feign indifference, yet I was dying. The image of an isolated Al Malbec noshing chips and dip sent me down a rumination rabbit hole for the rest of the day.

ᵹ ☙

The distractions caused by my preoccupation with my doctor forced another veil of malaise to settle over my marriage. We didn't fight angrily; the passion just fizzled and we stopped trying. I asked JD to give me some space, which he reluctantly did. He packed a bag and spent a few nights at his parents' home.

On my second night without him, I went out to the community set of mailboxes near the curb. On top of the bills, I discovered a small card. My stomach flipped when I saw the name on the return address: Malbec. I stuffed the envelope inside my jacket and ran over the snowpack back to the house. Once inside my bedroom, I carefully opened the note. The front displayed a heart design. Inside, he had handwritten a message: COLLEEN, THANKS SO MUCH FOR THE FANTASTIC OUTFIT FOR THE BABY. SO MANY PEOPLE HAVE BEEN FANTASTIC IN THIS VERY SPECIAL TIME. IF WE COULD JUST GET HIM TO SLEEP! THANKS AGAIN, AL.

I giggled at his use of the same adjective twice. I would have been thrilled by a lot less than the personal touch he put forth.

JD and I were in a sad place and hadn't exchanged Valentine's Day cards that year. I placed the thank-you note in my jewelry box and attached enormous significance to the heart on the front. He wasn't wrong to send it; it showed thoughtfulness and kindness, but the timing proved unfortunate. It reinforced my imaginary relationship, and my make-believe valentine became Al Malbec.

JD returned from his brief requested exile more confused and hurt than when he'd left. He refused to believe we had reached a precipice, like I contended. I declined to mention the card from Malbec. Without actually working on our issues, we both settled in for the long haul. I chose to spend my nights on the pullout sofa bed in the family room.

ᵹ ☙

That March, my first college roommate, Debbie, invited me to a gathering at her house with some of the other sorority sisters. They had been getting together over the previous few years to watch prime-time TV soap operas. I eagerly accepted, as another outlet for fulfilling my craving for healthy adult interactions. Getting reacquainted with the gang lifted my spirits and after a few weeks, I waded into the subject of my "cute gynecologist." I tried to put a humorous spin on the stories to hide the reality that the attachment had become an issue threatening my marriage.

Dynasty had started to fade, so we switched to watching *Moonlighting* with Cybill Shepherd and Bruce Willis. We laughed at the sexualized banter between them and found the show entertaining to watch. Secretly, it reminded me of myself and Malbec. One week, my friend Kelley came in very animated.

"Does your doctor have an office downtown?" she said.

"I see him in Edina, but I think so. Why?" I replied.

She gathered us in close, sidled up to the peanut M&M's, and started her story.

"So, I've got an appointment to get my hair done at this place in LaSalle Plaza. I'm bookin' through the skyways, making sure I'm not late. I'm pregnant, right? Running is not exactly easy. I get to the salon, and there's this guy in a black cape, reading a *People* magazine in my chair. He's got these pink perm rods in his hair, so you know he's not leaving anytime soon." Kelley popped a few candies into her mouth and continued, with us huddled in suspense.

"I'm super ticked off by this joker in my spot, so the stylist girl says, 'You're right. It is your time slot. The guy was feeling all self-conscious about his thinning hair. I told him the perm would give what's left of his hair a lift.' The guy decides to get the perm right then, during my time." She paused for effect. "It gets better."

No, I said to myself. *It couldn't be.* Kelley continued her tale.

"Then the girl says, 'You're not gonna believe this, but he's a gyno. Would you ever want to go to a doctor that hot?' Before I could think, she drags me over there to talk to him. He was chattin' about all the stars in the magazine who'd had work done. And I'm sitting here thinking, 'Dude, you should talk about vanity with your perm rods on my time.' The girl that does my hair says, 'Bye, Al' when he leaves. I ask her the guy's last name. You guessed it. It was totally him."

Everybody howled with laughter, both at the story and the telling. The callow jerk of a man she described was the same object of my adoration. I laughed along with my friends, but inside I became unnerved. In an immediate rewrite, I couldn't believe how lucky she was to run into him. Surely God and the Universe had conspired to put my friend in that place as a witness. I became convinced it was a sign pointing the way for Al and me to have a real relationship. In a fluid moment, I made a mental switch from knowing it was a fantasy to believing we had a future together.

ꕤ

At my next meeting with the therapist, she had me take the Minnesota Multiphasic Personality Inventory, an expensive diagnostic test that took hours to complete. I brought the test home and followed the instructions explicitly, then mailed it back to her. She ate her Chinese takeout in front of me as she relayed the results in her office.

"Your test came back valid. The questions detect whether you try to lie, cheat, or outsmart the test, and apparently you didn't." Her chopsticks clicked as she picked up a snow pea. "It seemed to reveal some dependency, but no mental illness or anything serious." I paid her for the session and the results. Of course, I had no idea what the clinical definition of "dependency issues" meant, but that part didn't surprise me. I was sure I wasn't a basket case, either; I didn't need a two-hour exam to tell me I wasn't crazy. The sessions with her appeared to be a waste of time and money, leaving me unsatisfied.

ꕤ

I stopped wearing my wedding ring as a form of silent protest against an institution that left me feeling trapped and confined. It felt rebellious in a passive way. Therapist number two had been fired, and we were no closer to understanding our communication difficulties. I still felt invisible to the world at large, with four children in tow, and had been married all my adult life. After a few weeks, I no longer noticed the ring's absence.

The earth was just starting to thaw toward spring, around April, when one of the families from playgroup threw a bon voyage party for themselves. They were relocating to California, and I promised I'd help the night of the party. JD didn't know them and showed no interest. He volunteered to watch our kids at home, so I attended the party alone. I set out snacks and cleared bottles from the family room. A man I'd never met engaged me in conversation. The topics were superficial, nothing extraordinary, from my perspective. When I got up to check out the kitchen, he threw his jacket on and prepared to leave. But before he left, he felt the need to shout scathing words in my direction.

"I hope it gives you a big ego boost to lead people on. You ought to be ashamed of yourself!" He glared at me, stomped away in a huff, and slammed the door.

"What was that about?" I said to the hostess.

"Jeff's boss is a little fragile. He was recently divorced. He wanted to ask you out, but I told him you were married with four kids. I guess he got the wrong idea."

Feeling foolish and ashamed, I left soon after the stranger's outburst. The offended man's words stung, and I walked the few houses home alone, trying to recall what I'd said to him. I internalized the guilt and decided I must have done or said something wrong. The message landed loud and clear: the ring meant everything. I was either in or out, nothing else.

Chapter Eleven

The Annual

"One more time," I whispered to myself as I pulled the white cotton tee over my shrinking chest. I'd gone from a breast-feeding D cup to barely an A. I had shopped extensively for the outfit. The houndstooth pencil skirt and wide, black, patent-leather belt slipped on effortlessly. In the four months since I'd seen Malbec, my weight dropped from 129 to 102 pounds. My nonexistent appetite aided the weight loss, and butterflies replaced the urge to eat. The constant hunger flutter in my stomach mimicked the feeling of being in love, and I reveled in it.

The shoes were the best part of the ensemble: black-and-white spectator pumps, bought solely for this routine doctor's appointment. A wide gold necklace, earrings, and my wedding band completed the look. After all the times I'd skipped wearing it, I made the choice to wear my ring that day.

I waltzed into the remodeled office like I was the inspiration. In mauves and tans, the space finally reflected the all-female clientele. Coordinated upholstered chairs replaced the shabby, outdated, overstuffed furniture. Seeing the revamped space, I felt energized and excited.

"Hey, skinny, I almost didn't recognize you. How are you?" he said, walking up to me with arms outstretched.

"Nice to see you," I replied, the understatement of the year. I heard a phone ring. The strange timing sounded like the call came from in house.

"Line one, Dr. Malbec," a nurse said.

"Okay, I'll be right there." He turned to reach for my arm, but missed. "Go ahead into Exam One, and I'll be in there in a minute."

With the door closed, I began to unbuckle my belt. He knocked and entered in one motion.

"Hang on, Colleen. I'm going out to deliver a little baby." This time his hand rested on my belt, as if it were perfectly natural and acceptable. "Can you come back at one forty-five?"

"Sure, I took the day off. But I'll need to call my sitter," I said. These were both lies. I couldn't take a day off, not as a stay-at-home mom. And my mother was not simply a babysitter.

"Wonderful. Get some lunch or go shopping. I'll meet you back here at one forty-five. You can use the phone on the desk. Just dial nine."

I called my mom to tell her I'd be delayed, indefinitely. I couldn't shake the feeling the delivery call was staged and the nurse was in on it. Ruse or not, I had to leave.

I went to Southdale, a nearby shopping mall. I hadn't eaten much in the past three days, yet my stomach still didn't register hunger. Instead, I strolled past a store for petites and turned in. I moved through the displays and gravitated to the round sale rack. It felt powerful to pull the size 2 and hold it up, knowing it'd actually fit. I'd never been that size in my adult life. I overheard the salesclerks discuss my shoes. I wanted to be mistaken for a career woman on her lunch break, not a masquerading housewife looking for cheap thrills with her doctor. They both cooed over the pumps. I bought nothing.

Back at the doctor's office, the nurse took me directly to the exam room, where I disrobed. With a quick knock, he returned and entered my room. I found it interesting he wore the same clothing: a nice dress shirt and tie, a pair of suit pants, and his lab coat. I'd assumed he'd have changed for the delivery. More evidence he'd faked the whole thing. He put his hands behind his back, resting them on the doorknob.

"It's a wonderful day. I had lunch with my wife," he said with a smile.

The statement confused me. What about that made the day

wonderful? My distrust drew me to imagine wildly improbable scenarios. He'd engineered the fake call and used the opportunity to tell his wife about us. Just as quickly, I dismissed the notion and became angry. *You ass*, I thought. *You staged an emergency in order to have a planned lunch with your wife? Did you tell her how you rubbed my naked back at the pre-op? Or any of the pet names you have for me, like 'kiddo' and 'dear'? Or how you wanted to cancel my surgery with me on the table?* My moods flip-flopped so quickly it scared me. I struggled to make the ambiance light and friendly without revealing my emotional lability.

"So, what did you have?" I said, purposefully vague, whether referring to his lunch or something else.

"A beautiful baby boy." He gave me an odd look, like, *You bought me a gift, you should know*. The room held an awkward silence. "What have you been doing for humor lately?" he said, finally.

"You mean Kicks?" I replied, a double-entendre reference to a local hot spot.

"You won't find love in bar," he shot back.

Why should he care about where I go? I was simultaneously thrilled at his protectiveness and miffed at the snap judgment of me.

He went back to his child. "I had a little boy in February. He's thirteen weeks and fifteen pounds."

"What was his birth weight?"

"February . . . Oh, weight? Seven pounds, eight ounces."

"Wasn't he early?"

"Yes, three weeks." It surprised me he didn't question how I remembered the smallest details of his life. We discussed the overfed child and how his demands weighed on both the doctor and his wife. I realized, despite his and his wife's advanced age, they were still new parents. The entire conversation took place during pelvic, breast, heart, and lung exams. He told me I was perfect.

"Do you have any questions?"

"Yes." Hesitant to bring it up, and unprepared, I had no

awareness how to phrase what confounded me. I swallowed hard and took a deep breath. "I told you we were having lots of problems."

"I know, I thought you were separated. I was surprised to see a ring on your finger."

The mood in the room changed. It felt like the floor shifted, or maybe my often-discarded wedding band held magical powers. Why did he notice? Maybe he noticed more than I calculated. All bets suddenly off, I continued.

"I hadn't worn it in months, but I had a bad experience. Until we work out our differences, either way, I'm leaving it on." I needed to wade into an even-dicier subject for me. "I feel really lost, and I don't know who else to ask. It's about my response. I've never had an orgasm. I'm not sure if we're sexually incompatible or what." Sitting in my paper dress, I held my breath, certain he was going to tell me I was clitorally challenged. Or it fell off in one of my deliveries.

"First off, I hear this all the time. I feel bad for the ones who never ask. Fifty percent of the female population is anorgasmic, regardless of what you read. Being motivated with your partner is necessary. Do you have any experience with other partners?"

I shook my head silently, suddenly feeling diminished, and wondering where this line of questioning would lead.

"I imagine you've expressed your needs. It's frustrating. It sounds like there could be some incompatibility there. Married sex is boring because you have to plan it out. Face-to-face in the dark under the covers can grow tiresome. I have no doubt your husband's satisfied. You're young and good-looking and thin as a rail. You're going to get snatched up." I'm not sure what was more red—my face or the flags he threw.

At that point he launched into a defense of his rushed marriage after his own divorce. He gave me the whole timeline, from being set up on a blind date to wearing wedding rings at the office Christmas party. I had no idea why he was going on and on except to explain his unhappiness at jumping too soon. By the end of the story, I needed a break. I shifted on the table, and he got the clue.

"I'll be thinking of you. You're fine. Everything is great," he said.

Knowing I may not see him for at least a year, I shelved my common sense and allowed my heart to take the risk of a lifetime. I put my right hand on my chest to hold up my paper dress. My left arm reached out to him. He stepped into my embrace and returned it. We held each other for an electric moment and despite all the strange twists the day took, it felt like the earth stopped turning.

"Give me a call," he said.

Chapter Twelve

The Meltdown

"Call me" was one of the worst phrases he could have said. The summer of 1989 radiated warmth. I could have enjoyed the kids, my garden, or spending time outside. Instead, I obsessed about when to contact him again and what to say. My journal became my constant companion, and I wrote two or three times a day. Meanwhile, the relationship with my husband deteriorated further. A frosty coexistence gradually replaced biting hostility. We moved in different orbits and set a date for August 1 to separate.

The night of June 5, a voice came to me in a dream. The voice reminded me of the same one I had heard after Will was born. It said, "In two weeks your life will change. It will be difficult, but you will transcend the difficulties." I had no idea what the voice spoke of, but I attributed it to my marital strife. Maybe JD would finally get fed up and serve me papers for divorce. I phoned my sister Maureen, so I'd have a witness. She didn't understand the dream any more than I. I didn't mention I'd heard the voice previously, but I wanted her to know about the dream in case something awful came to pass.

The dream bubbled up completely different from others I'd been having. Vivid colors and soaring vistas populated my nights when I actually slept. With very little food or sleep, fumes of sustenance were all I had.

Every romantic song ever written seemed to be inspired by my love for Al. I chronicled epiphanies and described irrational self-confidence and how all signs pointed to an eventual affair. Fantasies of picnics in the park and clandestine rendezvous in five-star hotels filled the pages of my journal. Thoughts of Dr. Malbec eclipsed all others. He had the gravitational pull of a black hole.

When Father's Day came around, JD and I took the kids to my parents' home to celebrate, along with the rest of my family. Despite our failing marriage, we felt compelled to keep up appearances. A glorious sun poured out beams of warmth in the pool area, where my siblings relaxed, clustered around picnic tables. When the radio blared Billy Joel's "Tell Her About It," it wasn't just background noise to me. Certainly it was a strong suggestion from the Universe, meant just for me at that split second; I heard the words clearly. I transposed the pronouns and decided Billy sang about telling Al Malbec my fantasies.

My mind tried to process all the feelings at once. Thoughts of Al were exciting. Guilt weighed on me for possibly ripping up my children's lives. Insecurity and raging overconfidence occupied my crowded heart.

"My marriage is in shambles and nobody cares!" The comment came shooting out of me without context. My brothers and sisters stared at me but sat frozen. My sister Pat told me Father's Day was not an appropriate time to air my personal problems.

"It's never the right time with you people. There's always a reason we can't talk about what's real. Maybe I should wait for Arbor Day. Would that be a better holiday, Pat?"

She looked down and appeared confused. It felt like my head was physically expanding or I was riding in a hot air balloon, but without a tether. Layers came together: losing my marriage and JD, how my family would accept (or not) my new relationship, my children's well-being, and somewhere way down the priority list, my own health.

A combination of rage, fear, desire, and sadness got put in a blender and emulsified. Finally, Dad came over to put his arms around me, and we both cried. He stood there on his one leg and crutches. I wanted to hang on him for support, but it wasn't physically or emotionally possible.

I hadn't seen or heard my dad cry since I was five. Muddled memories flooded my head. Dad as a younger man, weeping uncontrollably in his wet raincoat as I stared at him. It confused me, and for a moment I thought those old tears were for my current plight too. He kept saying, "I'm sorry." Today, supportive words or gestures didn't come from him, just copious tears and the repetitive apology. I wiped my face with the back of my hand, allowed my father to let go of me, and took a seat under the sun umbrella. No one knew what was happening; Dad had tried to fix it but could not.

I somehow regained my composure while I seethed. After a long silence, my brother-in-law said, "Have you seen my new bathing suit?" The party continued as if my odd outburst had never occurred.

ꕤ ꕤ

Monday arrived and I rose after less than two hours of sleep. My thoughts raced, feeling like boulders crashing together in my skull. Almost effortlessly, I could recall separate conversations with Al Malbec I'd had over the past eighteen months. The amazing retentivity turned the mental transcripts over and over in my head and resulted in an epiphany. I convinced myself he had feelings for me that he couldn't reveal. At that point, I became consumed by an urgency to write him a letter.

Instead of choosing beautiful stationery and employing some cute rejoinder to his "Give me a call," I grabbed a legal pad and scrawled out something like this:

I FIGURED IT OUT. YOU ARE THE MOST WONDERFUL MAN ON EARTH. I'M SURE YOU'VE BEEN IN PAIN THINKING I'M IN LOVE WITH SOMEONE ELSE, BUT IT WAS YOU ALL ALONG. I FINALLY LET GO AND LET GOD, AND I'M SO HAPPY. WRITE ME A LETTER. ME.

I decided it was perfect in its impulsiveness, and I had stated everything I needed to without any further explanation required. With Will in the stroller and my girls following like ducklings behind us, we walked to the mailbox up the street.

I lifted the letter from my purse with one hand and slightly opened the heavy blue drawer of the mailbox with my other. After the plain white envelope marked PERSONAL AND CONFIDENTIAL and addressed to his office disappeared inside, I let the drawer slam with a clunk, the missive impossible to retrieve. My stomach flipped at the noise; a jolt of fear shivered up my neck. After eighteen months of secret mooning over this man, I decided the risk would be worth taking. Almost certain I'd done the right thing, I turned my back on the mailbox and my decision to disclose my true feelings.

The sun baked the kids and me as we walked past a vacant lot on our way home. Butterflies danced in the tall grasses, and I felt peaceful for a moment. Chores like a dirty kitchen and piles of laundry waited for me, and I took the walk at a leisurely pace.

Once home, the incredible light and airy feeling from the walk grew more exaggerated. I no longer felt moored to the earth and floated from room to room unreasonably happy. The younger children loved the fact their moody mother had spontaneously turned lighthearted, but Marni watched closely, seemingly on guard. We had a picnic on our deck, then I put the baby down for his nap and turned on some animated garbage television for the girls to watch.

Gathering baskets of dirty laundry from the children's rooms, I went into my bedroom to sort the piles. Conveniently, my machines were on the second floor. Even with the windows open, the sickly sweet odor of dirty kids' clothes assaulted my nose. The garish blend of neon blues, citrine greens, and every imaginable shade of pink swirled before my downturned face. It felt like I'd never seen colors that intense. In fact, all my senses were on high alert. The excitement built inside me as I anticipated Al's reaction to the letter. I lay down on my unmade bed and instantly fell asleep.

Marni woke me to say Will was awake. After a quick diaper change, I brought him to play in the toy-strewn family room. Hardly refreshed after my own nap, I felt disjointed and irritable. The four kids played in the chaos until JD came home.

"What have you been doing all day? The place is a sty. What's for dinner?" JD directed his justifiable anger at me, but I chose not to engage in an argument.

"I couldn't quite manage it today," I muttered, wondering why I hadn't thrown the white flag weeks ago. He ordered a pizza to be delivered as the kids danced around him, looking for his attention.

He went to sleep early in our bedroom, and I did the bedtime ritual for the kids. I read the shortest stories I could find. Something ominous seemed to be gaining steam inside my mind, and I could barely concentrate. The night hung hot and still, even at that hour. I pulled the hide-a-bed mattress out of the sofa in the living room, where I'd been resting at night, unable to sleep. Marni came down from her room, clutching a stuffed animal, and asked to sleep with me. I told her to climb into the sheets. She obeyed but kept her eyes open.

My head throbbed from the tension, and I began to pace. I tried to write in my journal, but I couldn't see the pages. The foreboding feeling kept getting worse, and now my mind felt like a clock wound too tight. Not able to find a release, I began to talk out loud to myself.

"Now what? Where do I go to get away from this pressure? Do I have anything in the house?"

I remembered there were a few tablets of Tylenol #3 leftover from my tubal surgery recovery. I ran upstairs to the linen closet, screwed off the lid, and shook one out. The blinding speed of my thoughts reached levels I didn't think were humanly possible. What was left of my mind decided the codeine might make me drowsy. With a quick gulp of water from the faucet, I swallowed the pill.

The decision to try a sleep aid put me into a yet higher orbit, and I became convinced of my imminent death. Worried I'd be found dead in the morning, I didn't want to have drugs in my system. I stuck my finger down my throat and vomited the still-intact sphere. I started to hyperventilate, and my heart caromed into my ribs. This is what it feels like to die, I thought.

A vision of Al popped into my head next: I won't get to hear his reaction to the letter. I knew he was somewhere in the world right then and as close as the phone. I needed to speak to him before I died. I ran down the stairs, into the kitchen, and threw open the Yellow Pages. I found the ad for his practice and the phrase "Telephones answered day and night." I picked up the receiver and shook as I punched in the numbers. The microwave clock read three a.m.

"Doctor's office." The calm woman's voice didn't slow down my urgency.

"My name is Colleen Durda, and I need to reach Dr. Malbec."

"Are you pregnant?"

"No. Please tell him it's me. He'll understand."

Ninety seconds later my phone rang. I grabbed it on the first ring.

"Colleen, what's up?" He sounded steady and alert. I heard his voice and wanted to cry. The words "I need you. I'm scared" never formed. Instead, I heard an extension open up the line.

"Hold on," I whispered to Malbec. I ran up the stairs to find JD sound asleep, the phone next to the bed on its cradle. I ran as fast as I could so the doctor wouldn't hang up. Picking up the phone once more from my kitchen table, I heard the telltale click of the extension again. It dawned on me it may not be coming from my house.

"Al, I've been having a really tough time," I stammered into the phone. My intention, to tell him of my strong feelings for him and my need to know if the emotions flowed from him as well, got completely thrown off by the eavesdropping. I veered away from what I wanted to say. "I thought I was in love with you and wrote you a crazy letter and mailed it. Now I don't know what to do." The words spilled out before I could gather them back.

The phone went silent. A horrific moment elapsed until he spoke. My future hung precariously on his response. "Maybe you could come into my office and we could talk about it." His voice sounded flat and emotionless. My split-second reaction told me I'd made a grave mistake. This man wasn't in love with me at all. I'd taken a leap of faith and landed flat on my face.

"I think it's a little late for that," I said. Then I hung up.

Chapter Thirteen

A Chat with God

Within seconds my brain imploded. Months of plotting and planning to get back to talk to Malbec ended in a sentence. My future decimated, I ran up to see if the phone really was off the hook. JD sat up in bed, wide awake. I looked at him and asked if he'd heard the conversation. But it wasn't his voice that answered. His face had become lupine, his eyes glowed red. I heard the monster that embodied my husband say, "I almost had you, but you got away. You made it." The beast looked evil and menacing. It snapped its jaws together and sneered. Fear shot through me as I tried opening and closing my eyes. The wolf-like creature looked straight into my eyes and said, "I love you."

I felt a surge of power run through my spine. "I love God more!" I screamed. I had no idea why I said that except I imagined I was in a battle with the devil himself. I flew back to the dark kitchen, my feet barely touching the stairs. I wrapped my arms around myself as tightly as I could and began sobbing and shaking uncontrollably. In the middle of the night, phoning a friend wasn't an option. I felt consumed by despair.

The voice I'd heard after Will's birth, and two weeks ago in that dream, returned. Neither masculine, feminine, nor human, it was more like a feeling; a *knowing* with words not of my choosing.

"I'm sorry you had to go through that. Soon you'll know it was all for a reason. Everything in your life has prepared you for this day." The main events and small moments of my life all flashed before my eyes. A lonely childhood, getting passed over for prom, the heyday of college, the births of my children, and the fantasy my real dad would show up one day because the one I knew had spanked me to the point of welts throughout my childhood.

"You see, I've also waited a long time for this night. You need a friend now, and so do I. I don't need you to worship or adore me. I want you to be my friend," the voice said.

Reality seemed so far gone by that point, I didn't think to question what I'd heard. I did what any professional nurturer would and reached up with both arms toward the ceiling to embrace the entity in my kitchen. The sky became visible through the ceiling and roof of the house. I saw shooting stars as though something momentous had happened.

"Heaven and Earth are one again because you accepted my friendship. You are very special to me. You are my daughter, and no one saw you; they were looking the other way. You are my second born. You are the Second Coming."

On a night that I should have curled into a ball and hid from the world, I became infused with joy. Not only did God talk to me personally, but I got a job out of it. Being a mother for nearly eight years and on call twenty-four hours a day must be the perfect training to save the world. Elation bolted around and sprang from my chest. I triumphantly went back upstairs to kick the devil's ass.

When I reached the bedroom, JD stood in his light-blue bathrobe. His face still looked like a wolf, yet the gruesomeness was absent. He asked me to be quiet, and I challenged him, saying it was a fantastic day and we should all be glad. I recalled the story of what God had said about me being the Second Coming. He told me that was impossible. Then I danced around him and sang a parody of the Mitch Ryder song "Devil with a Blue Dress On." I played my first-ever air-guitar performance and jabbed my finger at him while singing, "devil with a blue robe on." He wasn't amused, but for some reason it made the wolf head disappear. I went downstairs to call my mother. Surely she'd understand since she was the modern-day Mary, the Mother of God. Today was for the women.

My father picked up the call I meant for my mom. He wasn't about to hand the phone to her. He asked where JD was, and I said upstairs. He then said they were on their way over. I couldn't understand why.

When they arrived with Maureen, the last shadows of darkness clung to the kitchen walls. I went straight to my sister and said, "Remember the dream? It was two weeks ago last night. This is it! This is what the dream meant." She looked at me with the first pair of tear-brimmed eyes I'd see that day. I couldn't tell if she understood or if she didn't. She came to babysit. No one was talking directly to me, but they were looking for a place to take me, like a hospital. I knew I needed a break, but I didn't realize I'd had one.

They made a lot of calls around to find a hospital with a mental health department. The closest one, Fairview Southdale, had no availability. Somewhere along the line, my family got the misinformation I needed to be suicidal to be admitted, which wasn't the case. I decided to let them work it out without me because I didn't need a hospital. I needed a hotel, preferably one with a pool. Grabbing a blanket to hide my pajamas, I sat out on a chaise lounge on my deck to watch my first-ever sunrise.

I smiled and watched in awe as the salmon glow on the horizon turned orange, then blazing yellow. The longest night of my life extinguished, and a new day finally dawned. "Did you like it? That one was for you," the voice said, making itself known again. Obviously, it had never left. This infused me with calm and happiness. Whatever my family chose for me, something bigger and wiser proved in charge. I would be fine.

I heard the door to the deck open and my father yell, "Get her off of there. The neighbors are gonna talk." I walked into the house with a flourish of my blanket just to spite him. He told me to get dressed. Reluctantly, I went to my room and picked out the lemon-yellow tracksuit I had worn to my tubal surgery. The color oozed symbolism: very Cory Aquino. My mother handed me the phone, saying the doctor wanted to talk to me. I held my breath.

"Hello?" A stranger started asking me questions. It wasn't him, the doctor I'd hoped. I decided to give the man an earful. "Listen,

I don't think sleep deprivation makes good mothers any more than it makes skilled doctors. But there's that rush when you don't think you can make it and you get that second and third wind. You know what I mean? I totally know what it's like to be a doctor."

I heard my name echo out of the receiver, but I handed the phone to my mother. Then I heard words that would change my life. I distinctly heard the man on the other end say, "Bring her in."

Now that my family had the green light, I waited for them to convince me. My dad took the reins from my husband.

"Colleen, you see who's here and who's not. That guy you called earlier tonight doesn't care about you. But your dad is here. I was there when you broke your arm, and I'll be there through this."

"That was Pat with the broken arm, Dad, not me. You were there for Pat. I've never broken a bone, just like Jesus." He wanted to yell at me, but he couldn't, not today.

"I had some of my chemo at Abbott." He continued with his head lowered like he was talking to an imbecile. I decided to keep my mouth shut this time. He kept up the coercive speech to convince me, but my mind went to the place he mentioned. Abbott Northwestern Hospital was highly rated for many specialties like cardiology, oncology, and wouldn't you know it, obstetrics. I knew nothing about its reputation for mental health care since I'd never needed any, but I knew that was where I was supposed to go. After all, I figured if the God stuff proved true, I could cure people too. Abbott it would be.

I went to say goodbye to each of the children. My son got a kiss on top of his head as he ate Cheerios in his high chair. The youngest two girls sat in front of the TV. Lauren was unusually quiet. I made sure to avoid the topic of when I'd return. Sophie, three, nodded her head slightly when I asked her if she'd be okay if I went to the hospital for a while. I looked around for Marni. She sat, practically catatonic, in our empty den next to the family room. I could tell by her eyes she hadn't slept all night. In the recesses of my mind, it registered she had witnessed my complete mental breakdown. The part of my mind currently in control couldn't grasp that fact. I hugged my oldest and tried to assure her it was okay I was headed to the hospital. She didn't react except to hold her stuffed animal closer and suck her thumb. Hers and our family's world would never be the same.

Chapter Fourteen

The Admit, Part 1

I expected a balloon drop or a phalanx of reporters when we walked into the emergency room. Instead, the busy hospital functioned unaware of my holiness. Mom presented my insurance card. The woman at the desk looked up at me over her papers. Her eyes became wide as if she had anticipated my arrival. I liked that. She led me away from my mom to a blonde nurse named Debbie.

Since I had a friend named Debbie, I took it as a sign this woman could be trusted. She leaned in toward me and asked, "What's been going on?"

"I think I'm here because my parents don't want me to get a divorce." Emboldened now that I was separated from my family, I decided the truth should be told. She wrote down my responses verbatim, and then proceeded to ask me some basic medical questions. I thought I was doing a marvelous job of remaining composed, until she asked me my doctor's name.

"Albert Malbec," I said as calmly as I could manage. She stopped writing.

"Dr. Malbec is an OB-GYN. I meant your psychiatrist," she said. Although severely compromised, a part of my brain registered the fact this nurse knew who Malbec was.

"He's my only doctor, and I don't need a shrink." I felt like she didn't get my real reason for being there, so I did something that surprised both of us. I bent near her conspiratorially and kissed her lightly on the cheek. I whispered into her ear, "The world changed this morning and this time the women are in charge. We're in on it. And tell him I'm here." I sat back in my chair, gave her a self-satisfied smile, and waited for her to return it. I wanted her to realize I was God or at least show me some recognition. I also wanted to explain to Al what had happened to me. Instead, her eyes welled with tears, and I looked into the second pair of pitying eyes that morning. Not only did she not understand my message, but I was sure she thought I'd lost my marbles.

She showed me to a cramped exam room and told me a doctor would be right in. That is when I escaped from that room and went on my Savior of the Planet healing spree, until Sunny and the two security guards apprehended me. The elevator doors opened in front of me, and as I stepped into one of the locked psychiatric units of the hospital, Station 48, the unmistakable scents of fresh paint, drywall, and new carpet greeted me. The telltale signs of new construction surprised me in the old building. I decided an explanation would be forthcoming.

Images of horror-movie crones lurking in hallways and patients shrieking nonsense while strapped in their beds dominated my fears of what lay behind the locked door. In reality, most of the patients, in what appeared to be a common room, wore casual street clothes. The two who wore hospital garb, gowns and printed blue pajama pants, sat in wheelchairs, looking vacant, their faces slack. Those two never looked at me. They couldn't if they wanted.

I noticed quick, nervous glances from the rest of the patients, yet no one spoke to me. As I approached the long table to greet those seated, they slowly got up and scattered throughout the room. The sensation that my presence and energy lit up The Unit frightened and intrigued me. It appeared to me everyone moved in slow motion, shuffling instead of walking.

I moved through the open community room and gravitated to a huge picture window. I touched the double-paned glass, grateful there weren't any bars. Several green-and-white spider plants rested in plastic pots along the window ledge. I'd kept similar plants in the apartment when we were first married. This was a sign. I came to the right place.

Sunny called me back from the window. She turned out to be a nurse who specialized in psychiatric care.

"You're lucky you came when you did. The Unit just opened two weeks ago," she said.

The timing seemed more destined than fortunate, but I kept it to myself. She brought me over to the hub of The Unit: the nurse's desk. The woman behind the counter began my official intake.

She set my purse on the counter, opened it, and inventoried the contents, similar to being booked into jail. My cash, checkbook, and ID were placed in a manila envelope. I felt a slap of shame as I listened to her snap each plastic credit card from my wallet. She seemed to want to ensure I knew I wasn't checking into a hotel. On the contrary, my money was taken to prevent escape. It didn't occur to me I would be robbed if the valuables weren't confiscated. All I could think of was running away, but without money those thoughts evaporated. Finally, the woman pulled the laces from my tennis shoes and checked my pants for a drawstring. Since I came in with only the clothes on my back, she offered me a selection of toiletries and a toothbrush.

Sunny showed me around the rooms. Passing one of the televisions, I saw Phil Donahue interview a beautiful couple who had met through a matchmaker on a blind date. It reminded me of the story Malbec had told me about his wife. I moved out of earshot. When I passed the next TV, I saw a picture of Howie Mandel in his character's dream sequence on *St. Elsewhere.* In the dream, he goes to heaven and meets God, who looks just like Howie. *St. Elsewhere* was one of my favorite shows. Medical dramas were a vicarious thrill since my career as a physician never materialized. It's possible I hallucinated this entire montage involving the televisions, yet at the time, I took it as an actual happening.

My mind spun with thoughts of being God; I couldn't reconcile any other explanation for the events that morning. I certainly didn't entertain thoughts I might actually be ill. Without intent or a plan, I walked back to the desk.

"Can we get you anything?" said the nurse who had stripped my belongings and dignity.

"A bath," I responded, wanting to test the magic of the desk.

Surprisingly, she handed me a bar of Neutrogena soap (clear—to detect hidden objects) and a towel. I had the choice of a gown or pajamas, and I chose both, to represent the male and female sides of my Godness. All the bathing facilities were occupied, and I started to panic.

"There's one more option," she said.

"I'd take a sitz bath at this point," I said without sarcasm.

She gave me an exasperated sigh.

The nurse unlocked what appeared to be a utility closet. Inside were random chrome bars, portable IV stands, and a clawfoot, free-standing bathtub. I decided to roll with it. She brought some disinfectant and gave the tub a once over, then waited outside the door.

I half filled the tub with water as warm as I could tolerate, then slipped off my yellow warm-up suit and underclothes. A bright fluorescent bulb buzzed high above me as I set my head against the cool porcelain and assessed my options.

I started to fill the tub higher when I heard a knock.

"You sure you're alright?" the nurse asked.

"Yep. Just fine."

I sank my shoulders under the hot water and began to imagine my speech to the media. I pictured Peter Jennings, Tom Brokaw, and Dan Rather fighting for the scoop.

"It happened in Minneapolis, folks. We've received word the Second Coming is in a hospital, and we're trying to get an interview."

It calmed me thinking of the news people. After all, I had the confidence of being the highest-ranking person on the planet. Everything would happen on my terms. Despite those facts, I had no idea what I'd do after my bath in the closet.

The nurse pounded on the door and ordered me out as if I were a disobedient teenager.

The bath complete, Sunny asked me to join the other patients at a table. No one made eye contact, and I studied the faces of the people seated around me. Three men and two women busied or pretended to busy themselves playing solitaire, watching television, or listening to a Walkman with headphones. My brain reeled with thoughts maybe I had survived my own death, but this place wasn't my idea of heaven. I couldn't or wouldn't let myself begin to process any other evidence.

I wanted someone to connect with me, so I surveyed those seated at the table. I scribbled something down on a notepad and handed it to an elderly woman seated across from me. With crystalline blue eyes and white hair, she reminded me of my visions of what I thought God should really look like. She picked up the note and read it. "I have lived patiently in the absence of you." Her eyes grew large, and she pressed the paper to her chest. "But you're so young!" she exclaimed, with a nod toward the patient room closest to the space. She stood up in her housecoat and slippers, and I followed her. As I passed the threshold, I saw two first names: HELEN AND COLLEEN.

Randomly, I had given this woman the note, and the staff had already chosen her as my roommate. Another noncoincidence, I thought. The message in the note thrilled Helen. My heart leapt at her every word. She warned me we could only speak openly within the room because the staff listened to our conversations and wrote them down, whether we as patients spoke to them directly or not.

From then on, she taught me to speak in the code of the patients. Once, she picked up the phone in the community room and had a conversation about selling some stocks. She told me later the message was meant for me. She used it as an example of saying something with surreptitious meaning. It was a way to get your point across without saying anything directly. She also advised me to always order extra drinks for meals because the medications they prescribed would give me dry mouth. There was a way to act while in a group setting, and she taught me direct eye contact was far too aggressive. The conspiracy and secrecy heightened my mood, if that were possible.

She told me she'd often been in a similar state of mind as I but was now at her nadir. It was more code for "I was excited while she felt depressed." It took me a few beats to comprehend she thought we were in for the same thing, whatever it was. We were two sides of the same coin, young and old, thin and plump, but both beautiful and most probably, God. We got along famously. I again felt destined to be in the right place.

A geriatric man in dress pants, shirt, and tie approached me in the community room. A nurse introduced him as Dr. Silverman. This surprised me because he appeared past retirement age. How was it I had a doctor I didn't choose? He asked to have a word with me in my room. I sat on the bed and answered his questions without elaborating or revealing my real identity as Savior of the Planet. I described how difficult my marriage had become and how the only person who supported me in my quest to get a divorce was Dr. Malbec. Dr. Silverman never asked me if I was God, so I didn't discuss it.

He did tell me he had interviewed my mother downstairs. He explained since my family had a history of mental illness, I most likely inherited my condition.

"Excuse me?"

"Your grandmother was hospitalized many times. They misdiagnosed her and called it schizophrenia back in the 1950s, but she likely was manic-depressive. As I suspect you are as well."

A devastation waterfall cascaded over me. Why did my mother tell these strangers such news? And why was I never told? How could I have something like a mental illness? The abruptness of the diagnosis and his surety set my jaw rigid. I knew nothing about the word *manic*, and I certainly wasn't depressed. I also had six siblings. How could I be the only one to get this? Later, it became clear to me people sometimes waited years for the diagnosis it took this psychiatrist forty-five minutes to formulate. It didn't occur to me, at that moment, to consider myself fortunate.

I saw two choices: either I could believe Helen and my own evidence that something beautiful and wonderful had happened that morning, or I was hopelessly mentally ill. I would straddle that decision for the next couple of days.

"You will most likely be on medication for the rest of your life. It's a chronic condition without a cure but can be managed with close supervision." This new bomb didn't sit well with me, either. *I'm going to beat this*, I vowed. *The man just told me I'll be an emotional cripple for the duration of my days. I'm not even thirty. There must be some mistake.*

"Lots of folks have lived with manic depression," he continued, "like Vincent van Gogh and Mike Tyson." I reflexively put my hair behind my ear and wondered if he knew that wasn't comforting.

"I don't do drugs. I hate them. I barely take aspirin," I told him.

"We refer to them as 'meds.' I've ordered an antipsychotic, and we're starting you on a fairly easy medication to begin, called 'lithium.' It's like a salt." At that point he rose from his chair and headed for the door. "Do you need something for sleep? I can prescribe a sedative for you."

I feared sleep, and bringing it on willfully seemed the furthest thing from my mind. "Sure," I said quietly, in complete despair.

ꕥ

As darkness fell that night, the patients prepared for bed. I started to doubt anyone from the news media would show up to interview the Minneapolis Miracle. What if God didn't come to me and tell me those statements? What if there was no God at all? I panicked at both thoughts, and my carefully constructed defenses began to crumble. I jumped out of bed and ran to the door.

A small man with glasses sat crouched at the desk. After I described my dilemmas, including my sudden doubts about a higher power, he said, "I can't promise you anything, except I will be here in the morning. You have a sleep aid prescribed. Do you want it now?" Hanging my head in utter defeat, I nodded. I hadn't slept a full night in weeks and only rested a few hours in the last forty-eight. I had a cranium-busting headache and an intense, irrational fear of sleep. The male nurse appeared at the door several minutes later with a paper cup of water and a white pill. I swallowed it, certain I would perish.

From my plastic-coated single mattress with bleached sheets and thin blanket, I called out to Helen.

"I'm afraid to sleep. I think I'm going to die," I said.

"You'll be fine," she said calmly from her own bed in the dark. "I died last Wednesday. It's a snap. Tomorrow just say, 'Good Morning, Helen,' and you and I will know you made it."

Well, it had been a nice life, I thought, as I waited for death to come. I stared straight up, the edges of my peripheral vision darkened, and I lost consciousness.

Dawn broke early the next morning. The sun peeked through the slits in our stringless blinds, and I popped up in bed. If Helen was right, I had survived whatever metamorphosis occurred overnight.

"Good morning, Helen," I croaked.

She put her papery hand to her forehead, then smoothed her snow-white hair.

"See? Isn't it cool? Knew you had the stuff, kid. Let's go get breakfast."

Helen provided my lifeline for the next two days. We spoke at length and compared fantasies, and she gave me her number if I ever needed a friendly ear. She called me Piano Hands for a code name and told me not to stop dreaming of my prince, Albert or otherwise. I had shared a brief history of my association with Dr. Malbec. Her first husband had been named Albert, also.

She advised me to change doctors. Her doctor, Kevin Anderson, "got it" and would be better suited to me. I told her I'd think about it. Then came time for her discharge, and I became distraught. She hugged me goodbye, and The Unit went from daydreams and friendships to pills and drudgery.

❧ ☙

Most of my family of origin came down for a brief family therapy session. It was the first time a therapist laid eyes on the group. First, she objected to the way we referred to ourselves as "the group." She made an elaborate seating chart of the assembled collective, and remarked very astutely on how each person reacted to the news of my diagnosis differently. In a disruptive week, it was an hour that seemed helpful and appeared to shed light on our dynamic. Many years later, this same therapist would surface in a different capacity.

About two days after her discharge, I accidentally encountered Helen again. The light in her eyes had been replaced with a haze. Her beautiful hair looked matted and dirty. She was in a wheelchair, and in her lap were at least forty amber vials of medications, like she was being readmitted and brought her entire medicine cabinet with her. I yelled for the person pushing her wheelchair to stop. Helen's eyes didn't flicker any recognition toward me. She stared into space as the elevator closed in my face.

"Helen! I saw Helen! Where are they taking her? What happened?" The nurse at the desk told me, due to privacy concerns, she couldn't disclose any of the circumstances. It terrified me and made me doubt the truth of anything we had shared. My magic mania vanished, replaced with fear for what lay ahead for me.

Knowing Helen had returned but in a terrible state somewhere else in the hospital frightened me. What if I fell apart that easily? It was bad enough not having control over my own thoughts, accepting antipsychotic medications for the first time, and living in a prison-like environment. The invincible feeling of God's protective bubble around me evaporated. My time there seemed endless.

Unbeknownst to me, part of the reconstruction of my life while in inpatient treatment was to purposefully not inform me about privileges. When a patient was well enough, they were supposed to notice there were other possibilities for fun. I felt slow on the uptake, but I caught on eventually.

As patients, we had access to a beautiful, super-heated therapy pool, located in the hospital. No Jacuzzi; it was a full-sized swimming pool. I asked to go swimming, and by day four or five, the staff granted me permission. They had a collection of suits: unflattering, army green, and used previously by strangers. They served a purpose. The water, extra warm and velvety, felt soft against my skin. I swam with three other patients, but we stayed in our own space. My broken brain began the process of knitting itself back together. I felt less like a shattered Humpty Dumpty. Thinking of peace and tranquility also helped. That pool tethered me with a lifeline. It made me remember my exquisite humanity. During one of these swims, I remembered how I had wanted to stay in a hotel with a pool. I smiled for the first time since my admission.

Time passed nonlinearly on The Unit. Minutes hung like hours as I watched people I'd had conversations with come back from ECT (electroconvulsive therapy) unable to speak or remember certain details. This was usually temporary but disturbing. The two patients I'd seen at my intake with the vacant stares and slack faces were ECT recipients.

My sister Michelle brought me some brownies and gossip magazines on day six. The staff allowed her to accompany a group of patients and me to a local bowling alley. It was surreal, being out in public with mentally ill people, and being one myself. We wore street clothes, and the only giveaway was a sweet young man with two bandaged wrists, who'd attempted to take his life. Michelle's act of courage and kindness to join us stunned me.

With continued progress, I gained more privileges and went in an unmarked white van to a movie theater. We saw a Richard Pryor and Gene Wilder film that I would never have chosen. I stood up and walked out, fearful it would be the end of my passes. I explained to the staff member the extent of my anxiety and was asked to return to my seat and finish the movie. I practiced my breathing lessons like I was in labor, which allowed me to settle down.

The worst outing I experienced had to be the walk around the neighborhood. There was a sculpture garden and corporate campus nearby, so the staff nurse chose a peaceful, sun-splashed afternoon to take a group out. Three-quarters of the way, one of the patients started hyperventilating. She was having an anxiety attack, but none of the patients were aware what to do about it. The nurse tended to the stricken woman while the rest of us tried to pretend everything was fine. I felt self-conscious enough, like a circus animal on parade in the public space. Add the drama of someone's full-blown, screaming panic attack, and that nailed it for me. I wanted out.

I sat in Group the next morning in front of five or six other patients and a staff member. Two people had checked in and mentioned their goals for the day, and I noticed I couldn't visually focus. At first, I blinked a few times because I thought my lids were drooping. In reality, my eyes rolled upward until only the whites showed. The nurse asked me if I was "having trouble seeing." She took me to my room, and the next thing I remember were the words "Dr. Silverman, Call Station Forty-Eight, stat." I was essentially blind until she administered Cogentin intramuscularly with a syringe. The powerful antipsychotic Haldol they had given me caused the ocular crisis.

No one explained it, but I assumed the Haldol was prescribed to make me forget about being God. They didn't seem to have a drug in their arsenal to clear up the self-doubt, fear, and uncertainty about what lay ahead. Some combination of swimming, bad movies, meds, and the very structured environment helped me turn the corner and begin to make decisions for myself.

That afternoon, I remembered Helen's recommendation to use her psychiatrist. Dr. Anderson fell between my age and the older Dr. Silverman. I met with him, and he suggested a meeting with Dr. Malbec to provide "closure." With a mixture of dread and more dread, I agreed.

Chapter Fifteen

The Admit, Part 2

Pity is what I feared I'd see in Malbec's eyes. After my emotional train wreck, I wanted nothing to do with him feeling sorry for me. That would force me to admit I was on a lesser footing than he, damaged goods.

Feeling pejoratively about myself throughout my life, I really wanted the respite of being God. I was ready to forget the perceived slights I'd experienced and move seamlessly into my new role. Being Jesus's little sister, God in the female form, pleased me, and I decided I was well suited to take on the job. I had long been fascinated by the lives of the saints and often wondered, as a child, if faced with a miracle like divinity from God, how would I react?

I knew the voice that spoke to me each of those times, after Will's birth, in the dream two weeks earlier, and throughout the night before my hospitalization, was God. I felt so certain, I struggled with where the voice went and when it would return. What was I supposed to do in the meantime?

There were some sticking points to being God as well. If I really thought about it, I didn't know too many male egos capable of or willing to handle being in a relationship with a female deity. And if I had to give that role up, I would need someone compassionate enough to deal with mental illness. Temporarily, that person would have to be JD.

I knew Malbec wasn't really an option for me and at the same time hadn't given myself time or space to process the loss of my fantasy. Clinging to the idealized version of Malbec soothed my shredded psyche. I had no interest in being judged by the real man. To make matters worse, I had no idea when or if he'd show.

Simultaneously, I had to prepare myself for the meeting with Malbec and go about my other tasks as if it weren't happening. This caused one of those compartmentalizing events where part of my brain ran the Malbec scenarios while the other parts attended group therapy, ate meals, took meds, and watched the clock.

With the switch to Dr. Anderson came some time with a third-year medical student doing his psych rotation. It thrilled me because it meant I would be the subject of a paper and get pulled out of Group for interviews. John did a thorough job taking my history until he asked me about my "decompensation."

"My what?"

"Oh, sorry." He winced at his error, and the use of medical jargon. "Please describe what you saw and heard the night before you were admitted." When I got to the part about my husband turning into a wolf, I saw beads of sweat form on his nose. He maintained his professionalism much better than I expected.

The only time I felt disappointed, he pulled rank and told my friends to go home. My college friends Kathy, Kelley, and Nancy had come to visit me during one of his interviews. All I saw were their beautiful faces at my door. They came without thought to their own fears, straight to the locked ward. The hospital wasn't near anybody's house or work, and they had paid to park. They left gifts, which I opened later that day. What do you get a friend who loses their mind? Earrings, flowers, and cards. I wept.

The loneliness encased in self-pity I experienced allowed me to feel lousy and more like the me I knew. Even though the feelings were negative, I understood for the first time in weeks what congruent, appropriate reactions were. I stopped guessing how to feel and accepted the "bad" feelings as honest.

Interactions with the staff were hit or miss. A nurse told me I had a plastic smile on my face when I had nothing to be happy about. He used to tease me: "Is that Dr. Malbec I just heard paged?" This really bothered me because I had never discussed Malbec with him. He had read it in my chart and mocked me with the remark. One day he thought he'd engage the patients in a Trivial Pursuit game. When I got six questions in a row correct, he must've decided I could hold my own, and moved on. But this didn't prevent him from continuing to harass me.

One of my favorite nurses turned out to be a young man. He shared with me his true passion was his rock band, and he worked in the psych ward to make money between gigs. He seemed kind and told me helpful information no one else had mentioned. The only events between me and the door home were a meeting with Malbec and a turn in The Chair.

It never occurred to me to volunteer for the type of therapy offered in that room. Whenever I walked past the closed door, I heard yelling, shrieking, and crying. It sounded like torture. By then I had been in nine days. I would do anything to get out. I told the front desk I'd take the next opening available for Scream Therapy, as the patients called it. They scheduled me for the following afternoon.

In the hospital, I normally snapped awake around seven a.m. Thursday, day ten, I mysteriously awoke even earlier, at six fifteen, with a strong desire to wash my hair. I showered, requested a hair dryer from the desk, and returned to my room with it. As soon as I switched off the appliance, my style perfected, a nurse knocked on the door. Dr. Malbec had arrived. He just showed up at an hour I would normally be asleep, without warning. I decided I had been tipped off by the cosmos, and it made me feel better.

I opened the bathroom door, and a young phlebotomist rolled her cart into my room for a blood draw. When she heard it was Dr. Malbec waiting for me, her eyes bulged and she became agitated, like she knew of his reputation and he would bite her head off. I assured her it was okay to take her time with the blood draw. Dr. Malbec was a friend of mine and paying me a personal visit. I needed to say that out loud to convince myself of the reason he was waiting for me. When she finished, I grabbed my journal for comfort and a nurse led me to a consult room down the hall.

I had no other clean clothes, so I wore a pair of shorts (with the drawstring removed by the staff) and a T-shirt to meet him. Chilled due to the stupid outfit and racked with nerves, I approached the door.

I didn't know what to expect. Seated in a chair next to a cocktail table under lamplight, he didn't seem real. An ugly cast-off vinyl chair sat empty in front of him, for me. As I entered the room, he rose. A simple gesture, but I felt respected. The nurse left us alone. It was seven a.m.

"My God, you're thin" were his first words. If he only knew he got the God part right, I thought.

All I could think of was the last time he saw me, in his office, he had called me skinny. It had been a compliment. Gone was my fancy outfit, and the surroundings here didn't help. I drank him in. I swear he got a fresh haircut. He wore a fabulous charcoal-gray suit with leather braces, a tie clip, a pocket scarf, and a crisp white shirt. He looked like he had spent days getting ready for this. I melted.

"I got your letter," he began. "I'm sorry if I caused you any pain."

"Self-inflicted," I said too quickly, absolving him. Damn, there was no way to prepare for this. I bit my lip, and I felt the clock stealing the time I had left with him.

"My doctor says I need to be adored," he began, unprompted. "He was at the Christmas party when my wife and I walked in with our new rings on. I'm sure my doctor thought, 'Here goes Malbec again.'" The story sounded so strange. Apparently, he was also under the care of some sort of therapist? What the hell? Why did he tell me this crap?

"I have to say," he continued, "I'm happily married, but if that weren't the case, we'd be talking about something else." What was that? I couldn't breathe. Slam the door only to open it again? Happily married, my ass. I decided he was trying to convince one of us. I had my own impressions of his marriage.

"I've been where you are. But mine was much worse. I had *an affair.*" He said it so lightly, different than the rest of his words. He continued to tell me the circumstances and how he had proposed to his mistress. She told him she'd never marry someone who'd been unfaithful. She refused the ring. Then he came clean to his wife, and she kicked him out of the house.

"Lost them both on the same day," he said. "I got really depressed." I assumed he expected sympathy at that point but, dumbfounded, I couldn't speak. My mind reeled with the revelations of his infidelity. And how he made it analogous to my situation. He continued.

"I don't want you to love me, then turn around and hate me." Now I thought I was lucky to be in the hospital. I was probably going to have a second breakdown, and since I was already locked up, all for the same price.

"You can return to me as my patient or you never have to see me again. It's all up to you." Still completely speechless, I watched him stand. I had lost my mind, and here he was, supposedly to provide closure. Instead, the door gaped open, and I learned more than I ever wanted to about his weird love life. I could only assume he wanted to turn me off, big time. Nothing else made any sense.

I thought for a split second of all the days and nights I'd spent poring over details of this man, and I would most likely never lay eyes on him again. His ambiguous statements and strange true confessions aside, I felt close to him. In an odd turn of events, he used me as his confessor. He said, "Take care." Impulsively, I reached out to him. I felt his suspenders over the smooth cotton of his shirt as I reached my hands inside his suit jacket. Heat emanated from his back, and I wanted to crawl inside his warmth and stay there forever. Freezing cold, and nervous my loose shorts might drop, I wrapped my arms around his rib cage. He stood there like an oak tree, stiff and unmoved. This time, no embrace came from him in return. My arms released their grip.

I watched him walk down the long hall to the elevator. Unable to digest any of what he'd told me, I prepared to get on with my life without the crutch of thinking he'd be a part of it. JD and I would make it, or not, but Al was completely gone. My heart felt cold, empty, and flat. My slashed, pierced, and dying fantasy faded as he walked away.

My room seemed light-years away, but somehow I got back there. A nurse knocked on my door.

"Are you okay?" she said.

"No. But I will be. I need some time alone, please."

"For what it's worth, you did a terrific job in there."

Her words slapped me. Helen had warned me: they're always listening and charting. He worked there. He should've known they would eavesdrop. Maybe we were watched also. One reason he'd refused my embrace. Why did he share such personal information with me in that setting? There was no time for tears or brooding on any more details.

The staff asked me to go to occupational therapy and bake chocolate chip cookies with some other patients. The therapist's name was Michelle, which only caused a ripple of interest instead of gripping me like a sign from God. I noted the progress. The healing had begun. The rest of the patients figured out quickly I knew my way around the kitchen, and one by one they lost interest in the group cookie project. I continued alone, beating each separate egg into the batter with a vengeance. I longed for home.

That afternoon brought the watershed moment: The Chair. Verbal Group. Scream Therapy. Spiritual Exorcism. Depending on your perspective, my last hurdle had many names—the brainchild of a therapist named George, who loved the sound of his own voice. So much so, he made cassette tapes of himself reading meditations. These were offered to insomniac patients, for a fee. Since hardly anyone slept undisturbed, I found George's side hustle shameless and disgraceful.

George interviewed me for fifteen or twenty minutes. He told me the therapy, in its experimental stages, would take the place of months of standard talk therapies. Not knowing what I was in for, I gave him plenty of ammunition, but I refused to speak about Al Malbec. The therapist's idea was to provoke a psychiatric patient, using their self-disclosed areas of vulnerability. The best part? You had to have a crowd so the sensations of anger, humiliation, or whatever feelings percolated during the session would be heightened.

When I walked into the room where the actual meeting would take place, I saw a few nurses, a couple of patients, and my med student, John. Their chairs ringed the room. The Chair, reserved for the designated "volunteer," lay empty and waiting. I sat down.

"Colleen has chosen to participate in Verbal Group today," George mentioned for the benefit of the tape recording. I smiled at the onlookers, trying to imagine it was a twisted game show.

"You are just a peon; you mean nothing," George started off. "You don't deserve a real relationship. You're only going to be a housewife for the rest of your life . . ."

I started to squirm in my chair, uncomfortable but unsure how to react. "This . . . isn't working," I said.

"Well, I wonder why not? How long have we been at it? Thirty seconds? Listen to my voice," George said.

"Your father is the king. You have no role but to serve your family. And Pat is funnier than you."

"Bullshit! That's not true. You have no right to sit there and say that crap to me. God damn it, I hate this place. I want to go home. I do deserve a real relationship. You know nothing about me, you sick bastard. My father is not in charge of me. I want to leave this hell hole and never come back!" I began to release so much of what had been pent up. I continued refuting every prompt he threw at me.

Looking at the pebbled green carpet and nowhere else, I was unaware of the room or my audience. George prodded me up and over the ledge I had refused to go near since I stepped onto The Unit. My throat stung, my head ached, and primal rage continued to spew before I sat, breathing heavily, spent. I hated his smug smile, suggesting he and his evil methods had been proven useful.

When I finished, I saw John wipe away tears. He'd probably be chastised for showing real emotion, but it touched my heart. I wished I knew what got to him, but instead I stayed in the focus chair while the other patients gave me the standard "Good job," and waited to be excused.

"I'm sure it won't be long now," John said as he walked toward me. "Everyone on staff has been waiting for your dam to burst. You hold a lot inside."

"That's not gonna change anytime soon. I have no idea what's next, either," I said.

"Dr. Anderson wants to follow you after the hospital. He has a suburban office. You can discuss it with him," John said. His incredibly earnest face made me want to pinch his cheeks. There were very few professionals younger than me on my care team, and like Dorothy's Scarecrow, I was going to miss him most of all.

"Yeah, I'll have to look into setting something up. This whole thing still feels like a bad dream," I said. "I should wear one of those beauty-contest banners, 'Miss Mental Illness 1989.'"

He never did laugh at my jokes. With well-wishes for the paper he would write about my case and his next med-school rotation, I shook John's hand goodbye. Without hidden agendas or double meanings in his words or body language, he gave me the impression of a kind person and a gentleman.

Chapter Sixteen

The Obedient Patient

Rays of sun and naturally heated air enveloped my body as we walked to the car. Each step put distance between the unwanted memories of the hospital and my unwritten future. The sedative effects of major tranquilizers and mood stabilizers blunted my reactions to seeing my children for the first time in thirteen days. My baby didn't know me when I walked into the foyer of my own house. His big blue eyes stared at me, and I spoke to him, but he curled close to my mother. Once he saw me interact with the girls in the kitchen, something about the room made the connection for him. He squealed in recognition, both arms outstretched to me. I'd carried him since before birth, but lifting his weight felt more like fifty pounds than his actual twenty-five. My arms, weakened by inactivity and the psychic pain of my ordeal, almost gave way. I reluctantly handed him over to JD.

The girls presented me with wrinkled drawings of flowers and rainbows. Joyous bedlam broke out as I looked around my sunny kitchen with the white ceramic-tile floors. It appeared transformed, back to a haven. The last time I'd seen it, I had been God's selected savior.

I needed a nap and my own bed. I climbed the stairs and lay on top of the comforter, relishing its plushiness and the scent of fabric softener instead of the hospital's disinfectant smell. Sinking into the dream-like cushiony warmth of my own pillow evoked sheer bliss and unrelenting gratitude.

My village departed while I slept that day. Tough to blame them; they had coordinated daily childcare while I was hospitalized for almost two weeks. Nobody asked me any questions the entire time I was away, and many people were enlisted to assist. Oblivious to the details of how it was accomplished, I remained humbled by everyone's generosity.

Since the manic episode had shattered "normal" for me, getting back to a routine as quickly as possible became my goal. A small, quiet part of me noticed how many people it took to step in and do what I did by myself. That should have clued me in to start small. Ignoring my intuition, I jumped back into full-time mother mode when JD returned to work the following Monday.

I took Sophie down the street to playgroup. When I tried to leave, she let out a wail worthy of an abandoned toddler. I mumbled something to the other moms about "being away from home a lot lately." I had no idea what any of them knew, and I couldn't begin to explain truthfully. Almost in tears myself, I grabbed my daughter, hoisted her on my hip, and walked home.

Later that afternoon, I sat huddled under my kitchen table, wondering what to do next. The kids joined me, thinking we were playing a game. Overwhelmed, with my personal and babysitting resources exhausted, I remembered a friend I hadn't seen in a while: Oprah Winfrey.

Every weekday at four, I could count on hearing "Here we go!" and she'd be there for me. Because I was already a devotee, getting back into my Oprah habit brought healing. Her consistency (she never missed a show) and ability to connect with her audience helped me cope. I learned to love the opportunity to cry. Whether joyful, painful, angry, or inspirational, the tears flowed almost every day. If at all possible, I kept that time for her five days a week. And she didn't disappoint me.

I wasn't so lucky with my paid psychotherapy. After my brief Icarus-like flight and devastating crash, I wanted to avail myself of every type of assistance. Thinking if we threw ourselves into the world of professional help, we'd fix whatever was broken, JD and I started marriage counseling yet again.

"Let's go back to the good old days. Before your relationship took a turn," said the counselor. He looked distractingly like a young Benjamin Franklin. I saw JD's eyes go wide with fright until they met mine. We both burst into spontaneous giggles. The therapist said, "What's so funny?"

"We don't have any," JD finally answered. "We got married so young. We never went on a trip together or even spent a weekend alone before the wedding."

"Then the kids came, and we just rolled with it," I chimed in. "That's probably what got us here. So far it's been fairly stressful."

We never discussed Malbec, finding the subject painful and too raw. With a dismal prognosis, the psychologist dismissed us a few sessions later.

Concurrently, I'd been seeing Dr. Anderson for medication management and a woman he referred me to for psychotherapy. She fell asleep during the first two sessions. I tried a different woman. We eventually clashed after she deemed my relationship with Dr. Malbec "insignificant" and "unfortunate." Frantic and desperate after two failed attempts, I agreed to accept Dr. Anderson's offer to provide both meds and personal counseling.

He assured me of his prowess concerning the sensitive sexual arenas I needed to explore. I had my doubts, intuitively sensing something not quite right about him, yet I felt compelled to defer to his expertise. Choosing a heterosexual male therapist to deal with issues of attraction felt like bringing a flaming torch into a dark cave to detect methane.

A deeper dive into my history revealed disturbing trends regarding some of the male figures. I described the relationship with my father and the almost nightly spankings, with the requirement my sister and I pull our own pajama bottoms down before he'd strike us. Dr. Anderson pointed out how unhealthy and sexualized it sounded, and how it affected my self-image. I hated the spankings, but like a lot of kids, I wrote off the trauma and internalized the effects.

I had dismissed the welts I received from my dad in order to make sense of the rest of our relationship. "Believe what I say, not what you feel" became the mantra governing most of my life, especially the relationships with men. I had used those words to deal with the flick on my butt, the rubbing of my back and neck, and the overly casual treatment from Dr. Malbec.

Once Dr. Anderson drew the parallels between my father and Dr. Malbec, I took it upon myself to go a step further. My psychiatrist also seemed to be exhibiting sexual overtones toward me. In the course of therapy, we'd discuss my suspicions, which he vehemently denied most days. On the rare chance he allowed the topic, he blamed my "out there" sensuality. When I told him I only wanted his help, he said, "You want a lot more than my fifty minutes."

He used his position of authority to convince me his feelings were my fault. He lectured me on being overly sexual. Confused and at a self-esteem low point, I allowed him to turn the tables on me. If there was sexual tension in the therapy, the subject matter, my outfits, or my personality were surely to blame.

A year after my initial hospitalization, I admitted myself again, in the summer of 1990. I drove myself directly to Abbott from Dr. Anderson's office. At the time, I was having a mild manic episode, complete with a hypersensitivity to other people. I intuited Dr. Anderson had feelings for me he wouldn't acknowledge. He had insisted I wasn't well.

Around Thanksgiving in 1992, I attempted an ambitious wallpaper removal project in my family room to prepare for my hosting duties. Chunks of drywall came loose as I ripped the sheets of grass cloth from my family room at two a.m. I became distraught, both due to lack of sleep and knowing I was out of my league with the home improvements. This time, JD drove me to Abbott, and I checked myself in for a few days.

When I got home, I found the rest of the wallpaper had been safely removed and the walls painted by my younger brothers, Michael and Brian. I was touched by their kindness but couldn't adequately express myself at the time. I had come home heavily sedated, my feelings blunted.

I sat in Dr. Anderson's office months later and stared at the diplomas from highly esteemed colleges out East. Who was I to suggest this doctor was attracted to me? I couldn't shake the feeling while I saw myself as a mental patient with little formal education. All I had was a hunch, and I had been wildly wrong with hunches before. In his office that day, Dr. Anderson droned on about how my father's treatment of me influenced the concept of my self-worth. The effects of the medications seemed to inhibit my verbal expression of feelings, but words finally came to me, and I stopped him midsentence.

"Hold it right there." I sat up straight and looked him in the eye. "This isn't about my dad, or Malbec, for that matter. The creepy feeling is right here in this room. It's coming from you."

"If you perceive me to be like your father . . . ," he began.

"No! No more bullshit. I'm not projecting. You have a thing for me," I said.

His eyes looked away and he exhaled slowly. "Many psychiatrists and psychologists have been consulted about your case. The consensus was reached, should the topic come up again, it would be in your best interest to validate your intuition. You're an attractive woman and yes, you're right."

Too much truth cascaded over me all at once. *If he's admitting feelings, and I have this feeling about other people like Malbec and my dad, how right am I?* I had no opportunity to dwell on those facts. Dr. Anderson continued telling his story, clearly relieved. He admitted to wanting to go after Malbec for the way he'd treated me. For years he'd denied the feelings because he feared retaliation from JD or colleagues in his own field. And then the final blow to my psyche: he admitted he'd put me back in the hospital in 1990 for my own protection because I was so seductive. I'd never felt worse for being correct. He really did blame me for his feelings.

Still numb to my own power and ability to walk out, I accepted the revelation with unusual maturity and grace. Seemingly emboldened by my calm acceptance of his most closely guarded secret, Dr. Anderson doubled down on being helpful in subsequent meetings. We explored my dreams, like a recurring one I'd had that he and I went to Paris. One of the ground rules was to keep sexual content out of the descriptions.

"L'Arc de Triomphe stood majestically over the city. It was winter because we had on wool coats and scarves," I began. Dr. Anderson interrupted me quickly:

"Did we have sex?"

"You told me to skip that part, remember?" I said.

"Well," he sputtered, "if we did, I think it's germane to the therapy."

My intuition signaled me with a tightening in my chest. It felt like he wanted to hear me describe it, for reasons very untherapeutic. I hesitated.

"No, it wasn't like that. You were a banker, and I was there as an interpreter for your business meetings," I said.

From my side of the desk, he appeared disappointed. I tried to be obedient, to dig deep into my psyche for insight into my myriad issues. Yet reflexively, I felt compelled to care for Dr. Anderson's ego needs. It required a heavy lift on my part. Conflicted and unsure, I struggled to finish the session.

He sat there, in suit pants two sizes too small, and I articulated the rest of the dream. There was no sexual encounter to omit, so I described the sights and sounds of my imagined French capital. Maybe he would find Freudian significance in the vivid details. I still wanted to trust him.

Every previous visit, he would button his suit coat, click his pen, and stand up to open his office door at the end of my session. He would shut the door to prepare for the next patient. It was our ritual. That didn't happen after I concluded the dream sequence. I rose after glancing at my watch, and I saw Dr. Anderson adjust his clipboard over his crotch. He half stood, smiled weakly, and sat back down. Sickened by what surely was an erection, I left the office, pulling the door closed behind me.

I went back another time, but only to tell him I'd decided to terminate therapy.

Dr. Anderson freaked out. He insisted I see his colleague before I go. The woman grilled me and suggested I had fabricated an accusation against Dr. Anderson, because he had since retracted all the statements he'd made in the previous sessions about being attracted to me. It was tantamount to an assault. Shaken, I terminated all contact with Dr. Anderson. Two months later, I was hospitalized for the fourth time in four years.

Instead of solace, I found Abbott a changed place. Three patients named Al walked the halls, one of whom was quite ill. He looked at me through long, matted hair and said, "Absence makes the heart grow fonder." This was not helpful to my fragile hold on reality. He followed me around The Unit, wearing nothing but an ill-fitted hospital gown. I sought refuge in my private room. When I opened the door to use my bathroom, I found all my white towels had been smeared with excrement. There was shit on the mirror and streaks on the walls. The smell overpowered me, but the greater damage to my sense of well-being was incalculable. I requested and received a guard at my door while I used the bathroom, after it had been cleaned. The rest of the time I was on my own. Very sick Al came back twice before they found a spot for him on another floor.

My psyche completely destroyed, visions of being God returned. I asked for Communion to be brought to me, and in an unusual coincidence, my thoughts started to clear shortly after I received the host. I mentioned I was feeling better to one of the nurses. She advised me to "quit talking like that or you'll never get out of here."

That night, I lay in my cold sheets and attempted to find sleep. I heard a disturbance in the hall. The page went out calling some sort of code in Station 48. A female staff person from another department came into my room and sat on my bed while the psych personnel took one of the patients to The Quiet Room. Without a reference point, I pictured straightjackets and darkness. That was it. Even if I wasn't completely healed, I had to get out.

Discharge happened via telephone the next morning. Since I was between doctors, I was assigned to an on-call psychiatrist. I did my best to impersonate a sane, cogent person as I spoke into the phone, and he responded, "You sound so much better!" Uncertain of his point of reference, I left within the hour.

Chapter Seventeen

Trying to Cope

After these terrible experiences, I decided the hospital was no longer a refuge. I declared myself well, despite occasional manic episodes. JD and I made a pilgrimage to Disney World a few months later, with all four kids, and we accomplished a blissfully uneventful vacation from a mental health standpoint. My beautiful family took on the ability to compartmentalize and enjoy their healthy mom on the days she showed up.

Like two anvils on a seesaw, mania and depression throttled my brain and disrupted our lives the rest of the time. I engaged a new, all-female care team consisting of a psychiatrist and a therapist. The doctor, Jane Grant, tried many combinations of medications to stabilize my moods, and I followed her instructions to the letter. I developed physical symptoms like vision problems, gastrointestinal issues, and severe headaches.

My therapist concluded I wasn't sick, simply spiritually misunderstood. Susanne suggested journaling the separate voices I heard, including God's, in different-colored pens. Uncertain how that would help, I sat in her deep armchair and took in the room.

Windowless and lit by table lamps, the brown, gold, and orange hues slammed me back to the 1970s. Susanne wore her steel-gray hair short, her bangs mimicking the straight line of her small, even teeth. I asked her what she'd discovered in Dr. Anderson's notes I'd forwarded directly. She tapped her fingers over her mouth, indicating an exaggerated yawn.

"The woman he describes does not match the one I see sitting across from me," she said. "In fact, the therapy notes are quite boring. If what you say happened, no one would have any idea by his records."

I reflexively tightened my jaw. Of course his version of events, the official record, would appear scrubbed of his feelings for me. She handed over the stack and allowed me to take the notes home between sessions. I compared my own journals to the visits Dr. Anderson had dictated. His notes were transcribed by an office worker at the clinic. The session with the boner incident was conspicuously brief and vague, and revealed nothing.

"I'd like to spend some time trying to process what the hell happened with both Dr. Malbec and Dr. Anderson," I said to Susanne at our next meeting.

"Sounds like Daddy issues to me. I think you should put it past you and move on. Maybe we should just make fun of his name instead. What kind of a name is Malbec, anyway?"

Despite the obvious disconnect between us, my lack of options kept her retained as a therapist months longer than she deserved.

The manias and depressions went unchecked in this environment. I suffered them at home, unwilling to return to the hospital. Ecstatic religious visits from God and frightening absences of faith where I felt deeply depressed each took their turns. I taught religious education during this time and tried to understand my faith by attending church. I knew enough to keep my volatile relationship with God to myself, and attending worship services was oddly satisfying in my state of amazing grace.

The depressions brought embarrassment and deferred feelings of humiliation not acknowledged during the manias. I couldn't find or remain in the "in between" by willing it so. My mind felt controlled by unseen sinister forces, and I had no ability to trust myself because I was inherently untrustworthy.

While manic, I told my husband we needed to be divorced. Sometimes I shared my plans with friends or strangers. During these days, we had an actual milkman deliver to the house. One morning, I surprised him at the door in my bathrobe and told him my marriage was over. Stricken, the man dropped off my order and hastily told me to consult a priest. He mailed me a bill and canceled the service the next day. These emotional slingshots were terrible for me. They also were devastating for the children, especially Marni.

She accompanied me to visit apartments for the eventual separation I was planning. In one instance, the building manager put my full name on a sign in the lobby. WELCOME HOME COLLEEN DURDA greeted us upon arrival, ignoring the lack of any lease. Unbeknownst to me, two of Marni's teachers lived in the building. I found out when one of them called me after seeing the sign.

"Hey, Colleen, I saw you're moving into Fountain Place. Is everything okay?"

"Nothing has been decided. Her dad and I are still sorting everything out," I murmured into the phone, deeply embarrassed. It served as a wake-up call and had the same effect as leaving my open journal in the school cafeteria. If it was humiliating for me to have my manic fantasies on public display, it must have been mortifying for a middle schooler.

I tried to minimize my shame by avoiding those two teachers when I visited the school. Regrettably, Marni didn't have that luxury. My daughter couldn't simply avoid the disconnected images she'd witnessed in our house. Not long after accompanying me to look for a new place to live, she watched me pack for a vacation to Hawaii with JD. He'd won the trip and we went, despite my chaotic mind. This happened without any explanations to my eldest daughter.

The guilt from this type of miserable parenting on my part added to the woes I couldn't verbalize. I felt it on some level, but there wasn't any access to the shame it produced. No skills in my toolbox allowed me to grasp the bigger picture. Amidst my family or in my own mind, the only pathways to my brain seemed to be divergent: as God's very special friend or as a worthless mentally ill woman who shouldn't even be there.

Coping during this time took on a do-it-myself quality out of necessity. The insanity would be near constant, and I didn't have the luxury to turn it off and still care for my children and run my household. Mental illness for me revolved around associations. Everything had hidden meaning, interconnectedness, and messages from God. I tasked myself to sort these out with a personal method I developed.

One avenue to cope involved music, but it became a double-edged sword. I found comfort in the creativity of a song's expression. Awareness that what I heard differed from others' experiences crept up on me slowly. Bands like U2 exploded my soul instead of providing entertainment. I would listen for hours. My brother Michael helped me during this time. I called on him to play DJ and make me playlists. His curated songs soothed my psyche instead of allowing me to follow my own tendency toward incendiary choices.

Another illustration of going deep was the significance of Ruth. I tried a beginner's Bible study in an attempt to gain comfort from a source a lot of "normal" people used. The first assignment was a brief passage in the short book of Ruth. I read it through and found a few unexpected gems. The character Orpah, which originated Ms. Winfrey's name, jumped out at me first. Then I learned Ruth was Jesus's ancestor on his mother's side, which made her one of his grandmothers. I discovered one of my friends and Princess Diana had grandmothers named Ruth. I wanted a grandma named Ruth as well.

My maternal grandmother's name, Evelyn, I connected to as a form of Eve. That resonated with me. Then I looked closer and said her maiden name with a French accent, Root. That's how to pronounce Ruth, with a hard *t*! When I discovered her birthday fell on February 22 (2/22), it became even more fortuitous. I was the second born of a second born and, depending on the day, the second child of God.

When we were trying to decide how to pay for our anniversary dinner that year, JD won a gift certificate to Ruth's Chris Steak House. This was one of many noncoincidences I chalked up to my magical thinking and coping mechanisms. Desperate for validation of my methods, I told my mom about my discovery.

"Ruth is actually an insignificant book of the Bible," came her reply.

"But don't you see? Everything fits together perfectly. I could've searched the whole thing to find Oprah's namesake, and she's in the first place I looked. It's a sign."

"Colleen, nobody cares about Ruth. It's short and not nearly as prominent as the Gospels. And besides, you shouldn't read the Bible. It's much too complex for you."

I didn't quite believe what my mom told me, but it cast enough self-doubt.

ꕥ ꕥ

My imagination came in handy trying to deal with other aspects of my illness. My hallucinations were not just auditory; I saw ghosts flying around the ceiling of my bedroom. Whether my eyes were opened or closed, there they were. They seemed to be happy I could see them, to sense their presence. I tried to discern what possible message they had for me. I actually felt compelled to communicate with them, but then I finally made a decision they had to go. I scolded them telepathically and told them to leave my house. With no one there to tell me I was wrong to talk to the spirits or that it wouldn't work, that's what I did. There also was no book I knew of to deal with such a dilemma. Acknowledging the visions and dealing with them the only way I could proved effective. They left.

Sleeping dreams also elicited problems. Wild and grandiose, manic thoughts would materialize as I slept. I dreamt of saving the world nightly. As I solved situational puzzles and achieved levels of awareness, an unseen chorus would cheer my abilities. I'd wake up, simply a housewife and a mom. This caused momentary disillusionment at not being publicly powerful, then immense gratitude I'd experienced only a dream.

Curtailing an almost constant sensation of expectation took more effort. A feeling that something wonderful, like a surprise party, lurked just around the corner hung on for weeks at a time. Irritation finally took over because no party materialized. Anticipating one simply proved illness had returned. I became inured to the heightened sensations and learned to live with them.

Aspirations of fame, fortune, and extreme philanthropy became common too. It took a lot of concentration to realize how dangerous it was for me to dwell in realms not grounded in reality. The euphoria, addictive and amazing, brought a sensation of invincibility as well. Winning the lottery, whether the Powerball jackpot or as God's selected savior, definitely felt inevitable.

Denying the perception of good fortune became essential, and counterintuitive. Killing my dreams not only hurt the unrealistic but tamped down most of my ambitions as well. Striving and wishing for happiness fell off my radar out of necessity.

I used grounded, mundane occurrences to my advantage. I loved the sound of train whistles. In the middle of the night, when I couldn't sleep, I'd imagine the short and long blares were messages from a favorite uncle who had passed away. It calmed me to think he could send me a code to help me with my insomnia. Imagining I had assistance in another realm made me feel less alone with my thoughts.

The colors green and purple together were a sign God watched out for me. I enjoyed finding random pairings of the colors, like on the printing of my Target receipt and discreetly placed in ads. Combinations of the number two, like being the 222nd customer at McDonald's or a receipt totaling $22.22, also served this purpose.

Conventional wisdom defines this type of drawing significance to unrelated items as a sign of illness. Developing sometimes complex explanations for events helped me make sense of more consequential happenings. Craving validation and without the ability to provide it for myself, I made the next grave error.

I asked my mother to confirm my suspicions about my dad having inappropriate feelings for me. Light-years away from trusting my own gut and with my credibility in short supply, I foolishly allowed my mother the power to decide what to trust. Dr. Anderson had warned me not to discuss those feelings with my family, but with him completely discredited, I tossed out even wise advice. If my mother confirmed my suspicions, they'd be true.

I'd hoped she'd understand when I tried to describe my father's attitude toward me and how it left me feeling dirty, like it was somehow my fault. She didn't. My mother not only told my father everything I'd confided, but rode with him to my house.

"Why would you ever say such garbage to your mother?" my father started in on me. My mother sat passively looking away from me. "Your mother has done everything for you, and now you do this to her? Who do you think you are?" He stood on crutches with his one leg, screaming in anger. "You are dead wrong, Colleen. Now apologize to your mother for upsetting her with your lies."

The tension in the room made my head feel filled with helium. Dr. Anderson had been right about one thing. I had been naive to think all I had to do was tell my truth and a positive outcome could happen. On an average day, I had a difficult time combatting my father's controlling tactics. That day, my mind in a heightened state, I had no debate skills. I knew I had to get away from my father. I asked Mom to drive us to a nearby park, where we could talk alone.

I explained in more detail what Dad had said and done over the years. He'd seemed jealous of my dates or teased me about being liked by certain boys. Crude comments about me "parading" around our swimming pool in a bikini. I'd only had one dad, and he was my baseline for normal fatherly behavior. I never realized it wasn't like that for other girls. My sisters always wore T-shirts over their swimsuits, yet Dad's weirdness was never discussed among his daughters. When I got into therapy to discuss Dr. Malbec, and eventually realized Dr. Anderson had the same issue,

I came to the conclusion it was all eerily familiar. I'd lived with sexualized authority my whole life, had I known what to call "that creepy feeling someone who was supposed to take care of me was actually turned on by me."

My mom disagreed. With me, my conclusions, and my reporting; all wrong.

"That's what you wished happened," she said, looking right at me.

In my wildest nightmares I never imagined a response like that. She wouldn't even consider the possibility. Mom drove us back to my house, where Dad waited. I mustered the last of my courage and asked him a question.

"Did you spank me to the point of welts as a little girl, or did I imagine that too?"

He laughed. With a smile on his face he said, "Yes, I did."

Vivid memories of the demeaning ritual smoldered in my brain. At that point he considered the subject closed, my accusations discredited by my chronic illness.

This cycle of intuition, insight, checking it out, denials, and eventual gaslighting was the formula that fueled my bipolar disorder. I had zero ability to trust myself or find balance. My thinking became very black and white, up or down, the healthy gray areas completely out of reach.

ℰ𝒪 𝒪ℛ

After the debacle with my parents, I spiraled up even further. That night, at a Timberwolves basketball game JD and I attended, I thought there would be a big announcement that I was in the audience. And like other times, regardless of evidence to the contrary, Dr. Malbec would come to rescue me. It didn't matter what I considered him while sane; the fantasy of the man as madly and passionately in love with me made sense while I was ill.

A national production crew was at our local mall filming the movie *Mallrats.* False fronts, constructed over the actual store entrances, rendered the entire environment surreal. This exacerbated my escalating mood. I took the children to the mall, boldly walking through the sets. Somehow we missed getting into trouble. Part of my delusion allowed me to think cameras were trained on me at all times. I walked in and out of stores with the air of a celebrity, sensing the camera lens yet feigning indifference.

My mind jolted back and forth between cogency and insanity. The thoughts switched violently as if controlled by a faulty mechanism on a rail track. Within hours my ideas expanded on a grand scale.

Happiness flipped to euphoria, then escalated to delusional without warning. Like a slide going up, the path to mania became a thoroughfare to my brain. The symptoms broke through the mood stabilizers I took. The children were confused by the trip to the mall. Marni asked to visit a friend's house; she sensed my spiraling mood would lead to something more dire.

Chapter Eighteen

Spirited Away

"I can't find my daughter, and there's a camera pointed at my house." I don't recall the other statements I yelled at the police dispatch operator that day. The report I would later read categorized them as "bizarre." I made a second call to 911, minutes later, because I didn't think they understood I was serious. This time fear and irrational paranoia fueled a rant.

"Did you hear me? I said my child is missing. Remember Jacob Wetterling? When you hear a child is in peril you send everything you've got!" I screamed into the corded receiver and slammed it down on its cradle. Back then, every house—including ours—had a landline, making it possible for the 911 operator to trace my name and location. Even though my reasoning for summoning the police was faulty, I knew in my heart I was attempting to ask for help.

Within minutes, I heard the faint wail of sirens. Eden Prairie's finest came like the cavalry to my front door, despite the fact I was incapable of any coherent thought. As the first officers came through the threshold, I began to explain how I was being watched by a camera in a construction trailer across the street. They ran the plates on the trailer and told me it belonged to a contractor remodeling a neighbor's house.

Undeterred, I converted the problem to Marni, my missing thirteen-year-old daughter. Lauren, eleven, pleaded with me to understand. Marni was safe at her friend's house, and she had asked for permission to leave. At that point, the officer in charge asked another cop to take the three children upstairs. A different officer found my husband's business card pinned to the kitchen corkboard and called him at the office. The message I heard from the chaotic conversations had nothing to do with clandestine surveillance or my children. The real problem, apparently, was me.

My husband told them I had bipolar disorder and since the symptoms had returned, I must be off my meds. No one asked him what those medications were, or if it were possible the mania had spontaneously erupted. I contend the incident with my parents had caused the rift in my brain. No one was capable of piecing that information together at the time. Instead, they asked JD over the phone where I should be sent, and he told them: Abbott Northwestern Hospital.

In this moment of utter crisis, I splintered. A piece of me floated above the fray, observing all the conversations. I knew I was compliant with my meds, and our insurance had recently changed. Abbott was no longer in-network. But the tiny, cogent part of me aware of this could no longer speak.

Instead, the delusional, paranoid, and angry portion of my brain did the talking. I thought I recognized the EMT who walked in my front door. When I mentioned this, I saw a look of panic cross the man's face. He appeared to look like my cousin Bill. This was not possible, but the confused me yelled, "Billy!" across the living room, frightening everyone.

With one of my last semiclear thoughts, I desperately searched the entryway full of police officers. I remembered one officer on the force was a friend. He knew me and some of my kids from activities at school. I started stammering these facts and how embarrassed I felt to be seen by him in this state. Like everything else that day, it simply came out as gibberish none of the first responders understood.

At this point, they no longer addressed me directly. They discussed amongst themselves how I was to be transported. An officer went upstairs to ask the kids to find me a clean pair of socks for my bare feet. I guess the cops knew that where I was going, I wouldn't need shoes. The EMT backed the ambulance into my garage to avoid the growing crowd of neighbors gathered on my front lawn. Then they called for the long board. I wasn't going to fight them, but I had stopped speaking.

That was my signal I would not cooperate. Even in that psychotic state, my self-preservation and maternal instinct flared a final response. How could I leave my Lauren, Sophie, and Will home alone? I knew I needed help. But where I was headed gave me no solace. And worse, no insurance coverage. I did the only thing that I could think of at the time: I resisted peacefully.

Picturing anti-war and civil rights protesters from news footage as a child, I allowed them to take me out of my home, but I didn't go willingly. I channeled Jesus, Dr. Martin Luther King Jr., and Mahatma Gandhi as the EMTs bound my hands behind my back and strapped me facedown onto the long board.

I'll never forget the feeling of being lifted, first back and then up off the ground. My healthy body, with its compromised mind, was taken from my home easily. The board allowed the EMTs to carry my limp self to the back of the ambulance, slide me in between the sides of the box-like vehicle, and shut the door.

I don't remember hearing the siren as the ambulance left my driveway. I had no idea what would become of my kids or me. It shocked me how cheaply made and rickety the ambulance felt. The bumpy and jarring ride made me rock back and forth on the board. I tried to lift my head to see where we were, but all I could see were the brown polyester pant legs and one gloved hand of the EMT. After a painfully slow rush-hour ride to the hospital, I saw the reflection of the garish lights in the bay of the ER entrance.

The doors flew open and they transferred me to a gurney. I screamed for my children. My brain no longer separated into sane and insane pieces; the irrational part commandeered every thought. I was still in restraints and facedown when I saw a woman with a clipboard approach out of the corner of my eye. Her lanyard and ID badge bounced against her full bosom. The impassive look on her face made it clear my current situation wasn't going to prevent her from doing her job.

"I need to see your *in*surance card and ID," she said, emphasizing the first syllable and without changing her expression. Obviously, I couldn't produce it, but the EMT gave her the police report. They quibbled over how to admit me. I was fully awake, but some stretches of time and specific incidents remain blacked out from my memory. And others were indelible.

My psychiatrist, Dr. Grant, immediately placed a seventy-two-hour hold on me. This was the information I gleaned from the hospital notes because I was not apprised of much.

The admitting department got ahold of my now well-established psychiatric history from my four previous visits. They must've assumed I had the same insurance, because I was finally admitted and walked through the hospital corridors to Station 48. The only thing I remember about this part of the process was using the phrase "all that and a bag of chips." I didn't really know what it meant, but I liked the sound of it.

I had the distinct feeling I was being filmed. As if it were possible, this thought made me feel even more paranoid. I decided I was a princess and I owned the hospital. The staff and patients all looked like characters in a movie. I yelled these facts to the people in the halls. Nothing looked real.

I was in communication with an entity I thought of as God. This was a twist for me as I usually played the role of the Divine. With Dr. Grant's seventy-two-hour hold keeping me there, I was placed in The Quiet Room and discovered firsthand what that meant. I was deemed a danger to myself and others. In reality, the verbiage simply justified and documented their actions. I remember anger, fear, desperation, and supreme confusion. According to the notes, I had frequent outbursts and was "out of control." For my part, I just wanted to go home.

During my time in the locked, padded room, euphemistically described as "low-stimulation," I was offered Haldol to calm me down. I remembered eyes rolled back into my head, slurred speech, dry mouth, and a shuffling gait the last time they gave me that drug.

I refused it. I tried to explain that it was downright dangerous. Nobody on staff could decipher what I meant, so my refusal to take the antipsychotic was chalked up to "defiance."

Finally, many hours later, a man who looked like Woody Allen with a beard entered The Quiet Room. Heartened by this, I figured the beard made him a shrink and the resemblance to the director meant he was in charge of the movie being filmed. Worn down, I didn't know my name or whether it was night or day. He asked me some questions: What was the date? I quickly piped up the correct answer. Who was the president of the United States? "Grant" came the response. I could not recall my home address or remember the name of the hospital. Frantic, I gave the name of a competing hospital. They charted my responses as "sarcastic" and locked the door again.

I could see traffic out a window. I heard semitrucks leave and imagined they were filled with movie props and sets in an effort to confuse me. Lying on my back, under a bare bulb on the ceiling, I stared straight ahead. I swore the light was pulsating in some sort of Morse code, and I began to imagine God had found a way to subtly communicate with me again. I smiled to myself. There'd be a way out. The Universe let me know, "There's hope."

Alone in that room, I figured it out: there were other medication options. What they were offering frightened me, so I constructed an alternative. I knocked on the door for help. I requested Ativan and orange juice, a combo I used at home to help me de-stress and sleep. The Ativan was an antianxiety pill, and the OJ simply made me comfortable. Like magic, a nurse came with both.

Suddenly Woody Allen reappeared.

"Who ordered this?" he demanded.

The nurse looked sheepishly at all the people assembled and said, "It was in her chart." The Woody look-alike flipped through the pages.

"She asked for it, I saw the orders, and I gave it to her," the nurse said and shrugged her shoulders.

"That's ridiculous. A patient can't make those decisions." He threw his hands up, exasperated because I'd already downed the juice and the mild sedative.

"CUT!" I yelled. "I'm tired of this movie. I've had it. I want to go home."

The team filed out, and I heard the door lock again. I settled down on the mat and attempted to sleep. Apparently, the staff had run out of patience and called Dr. Grant. She began proceedings, which I was unaware of, to have me committed to the state mental hospital in Saint Peter, Minnesota.

Before that could take place, I needed transport to a different local hospital that accepted my insurance. Still quite ill and delusional, I left via ambulance. The orders to have me committed to the state hospital, something I still had no knowledge of, transferred with me.

It soon became clear all mental health departments were not created equal. Without decent programs, languishing in the community rooms all day was my fate. The routines at Abbott may not have been ideal, but at least the surroundings would have been familiar. Being a veteran mental patient by this point, I could tell there was a distinct difference in care. This particular hospital did not release my care notes to me, and my own personal journal skips this entire visit, so I have to rely on sketchy memories.

Around two or three days into my stay at the next hospital, I passed a whiteboard with my name on it. Underneath was the name of a Hennepin County judge, a time, and the words "commitment hearing." Terrified, I asked a staff member what it meant. She said it was necessary because of my "behavior." I knew I was impaired yet thought I'd been cooperating. Glimmers of lucidity were my only defense at that point. I could not process how to refute the hospital's assertion that I was dangerous enough to be locked up in Saint Peter forever.

My older sister Teri came to visit with my mother later that day.

"What's wrong with you? Why don't you take your medications?" Teri was aggressive, in a helpful way.

"I don't know what you're talking about. I've been taking pills every day," I replied.

"You're not taking something, and that's why you're being committed."

I stormed over to the nurse's desk to ask if that indeed was the case.

"Yes. According to your chart, your refusal to take the Haldol is grounds for commitment," the nurse replied.

Well beyond a light-bulb moment, a giant klieg light illuminated the circumstances to me. My fate hung in the balance of a sick game of Mother May I? I didn't know the rules or the fact I was breaking them. Here I was, falling through the procedural cracks. My life was simply another case for the doctor on call at this hospital. The shock of hearing the difference between discharged to home or to the state hospital was a few doses of antipsychotic medication hit me with crushing speed.

If it weren't for the fortitude of my sister Teri, my life could have taken a completely different turn. It terrified me when I realized how close I had come to being sent away. Even if the gruesome side effects set me back a couple of days, I'd do whatever I could if it meant going home.

Chapter Nineteen

A Few Good Years

With four kids in three schools, I had plenty of opportunities to prove my rehabilitation from the recent breakdown. I added Girl Scout leader, classroom art volunteer, and the cliché but time-consuming role of soccer mom to my résumé. I attended a meeting seeking people to run the elementary school carnival. I signed up to assist on the food committee.

I left the gymnasium that evening feeling deceitful. I looked fine. I was attractive, young, enthusiastic, and, most importantly, willing to help. What I kept to myself were the five occasions I'd spent in a locked ward. Remembering the fear I had experienced before entering Station 48 the first time, that inpatient treatment would preclude me from having a career or even volunteering at school, I chose to take a chance. I still had possibilities with the PTA. Nobody knew my history, and I wanted to contribute.

The committee consisted of the woman running it and me. Just before the event, she bailed out, leaving me alone. Without experience, I ended up panicking and ordering way too much pizza to serve the night of the event. The principal had to sell it for a loss just to get rid of it. Instead of the carnival being a redemptive moment for me, I felt humiliated by my mismanagement.

My mood percolated somewhere between irritable and embarrassed, looking again for someone else to blame. I was able to control it for the most part, but triggers lurked, ready to set off the spring-loaded trap. The two women in charge of the carnival summoned the chairpersons to the school a week after the event to recap. The women were in a jovial mood; the carnival had generated a decent amount of cash for the school.

"And now we'll hear from the food committee," one of the women said as she smiled in my direction.

"Well, there is no one else here but me." My voice grew louder with each word. "I got abandoned, with no idea what to do and no one to help me! It was horrible," I shrieked and screamed, then gave a menacing stare to every woman gathered, as if it were their fault. After a few awkward moments, one of the co-chairs put her arm around me, and I calmed down. No one said anything to me about the outburst. I finished the meeting and went home, shocked and saddened my foray into "normal" had ended so poorly.

Despite my outward appearance and desire to be like the other suburban moms, I wasn't. I knew it was time and went in search of a support group. The meeting was held in a clinic space, run completely by volunteers. We met twice a month, each time breaking into subgroups focusing on depression, mania, or family members of people with bipolar disorder.

The meetings were incredible. Not only was it helpful to have a pressure release valve, but the ability to speak freely to people struggling with the same issues, such as trying to blend into society, was invaluable. Eventually, a splinter group broke from the larger membership, meeting as a closed, private collection of high-functioning individuals. They asked me to join them. We met on the off weeks, which allowed me to experience both types of meetings.

There were about six of us, including some lawyers and physicians, and we were committed to supporting one another. My health improved with the exchange of ideas and not feeling so alone. I explained the dual debacles with Drs. Anderson and Grant. Someone in the group suggested a psychiatrist named Larry Berger.

Dr. Berger was an incredible find. He not only was trained as a registered pharmacist but also had gone back to school to complete a medical degree, a residency in psychiatry, and a fellowship in mood disorders. I appreciated his intelligence and sense of humor. With him on my team, I grew confident to try bigger challenges.

JD and I discussed the possibility of my returning to college. It came with risks of relapse and no guarantee I'd actually be able to complete a program. After investigating several different colleges and universities, Metropolitan State University, dedicated to nontraditional learners and financially feasible, looked the most promising. With the support of my husband, I enrolled at Metro State in the fall of 1995.

Counterintuitive and paradoxical, giving me more to do actually broke the cycle of manias and depressions. Adding coursework, homework, and commuting to my duties as a mom forced me to prioritize. For the first time since I was diagnosed with a mental illness, I felt capable and competent.

My first few classes weren't too strenuous because, for the first time in my life, I understood pacing. I had to budget my time and schedule everything, from reading to typing assignments. My classes also reflected an eclectic blend of liberal studies like studio arts, film appreciation, and creative writing.

My professor issued a challenge the first day of film class: write a letter to the Minneapolis or St. Paul daily newspapers, and whoever gets published will get an automatic A for the course. I reviewed the movie *Leaving Las Vegas* and mailed my letter to the film critic at the Minneapolis *Star Tribune*. I received a typewritten letter (complete with Wite-Out corrections) from him. The letter is a cherished memory as I was the only one in the class to get any response. Though I didn't get the fast-track grade, I still received an A for the class.

Not completely asymptomatic, I managed the mood swings and kept all my plates spinning. In writing class, we worked on a unit involving humor writing. The instructor had a stack of completed work in his hands.

"Where is Colleen Durda?" he barked.

I sheepishly raised my hand. He grabbed the top paper off the pile and laid it on my desk.

"Funniest thing I've read in a long time," he said.

Eventually, I honed my studies to declare a communications major with an emphasis in public relations. I graduated with a respectable 3.75 GPA at age thirty-nine. The moment I accepted my diploma in my mortarboard and gown was captured by the photographer. The self-satisfied smile wasn't just for me; it was for JD and my kids too. With so many instances of mental illness on display from me in front of my children, it was a rare chance to feel proud of myself and my accomplishment.

လ ဏ

The dawn of the new millennium brought visions of landing a sweet job at a public relations firm for me. I set my sights on what I considered the most important aspect: new clothes. Consulting my friends, I inquired what constituted wardrobe essentials in the twenty-first century. One kind woman, Nora, pulled me aside and whispered, "You need to get a job first."

Full-time employment was my final frontier. Clinging to the image of myself in a power suit, I looked to the show *Ally McBeal* to inspire me and dictate the norms of a modern work environment. Exciting coworkers, killer outfits, and big paychecks were all on my horizon. I combed the classifieds for the right position and typed up a résumé.

My brother-in-law called and said he was in a bind and needed an accounts-receivable clerk in the accounting department where he worked. He suggested it would be an easy fit for me since I was looking for work. With my intuition doing its best impression of Edvard Munch's *The Scream*, I accepted.

The fantasy of being employed crashed into reality. My new job was at a family-owned manufacturing firm. One of the owners admonished me for making "personal phone calls" when he overheard me talking to my twelve-year-old son after school. Expense-account lunches were supplanted by sitting at a folding table amidst vending machines. My coworkers called me Mamacita and laughed when I wouldn't respond to their catcalls.

The fact I'd never punched a "nine to five" clock in my adult life made the transition arduous. It turned out to be a change for our entire family. Marni was now in high school and suffering bouts of depression. Relying on other moms to give my kids rides to activities grated on my nerves. I'd always been there, in my version of reality.

When Lauren's high school color guard was invited to a competition in Chicago, I jumped at the opportunity to spend some extra time with her and signed up to chaperone for the weekend. The Friday we left, I noticed the familiar airy weightless feeling in my head. A blanket of unwarranted benevolence wrapped around me and the clerks at Target as I picked up some toiletries. Making note of the changes in mood, I still thought, *No, I'm fine.* It had been five years since I'd had a major breakthrough of manic symptoms, where the mania pushes beyond what the medications can handle, and it had never happened away from home.

By the time the chartered bus arrived at the high school in Illinois, I knew I was in trouble. There was a mix-up with our accommodations, and we ended up sleeping in the halls of the school and showering in the locker room. Seeing people's bodies lined up against the lockers in sleeping bags caused me to lose touch with reality. I became delusional and thought we'd been transported to a World War II concentration camp. It took all my strength to keep my thoughts to myself and force my mouth shut.

Inopportune tears and laughter seeped out of me despite my efforts to conceal the problem. Lauren and the girls on the team knew something was wrong with me, yet I was in no position to explain my mood lability, which could morph from happy to euphoric to melancholy and back to so overwhelmed with joy it made me cry. I withstood the rest of the field trip until it was time for the bus ride home. I wept quietly next to the window and thought about how unbelievably fortunate it was we had a bus driver.

One of the girls offered me her Walkman and a CD she'd burned that made her feel better when she was sad. Her kindness and empathy only made me cry harder. I listened to Elton John sing "I Guess That's Why They Call It the Blues" and bawled all the way out of the Land of Lincoln.

The bus rolled down the interstate. I looked out the window at the exact time an enormous buck lifted his head and stared at me from a stand of trees. I imagined the powerful animal sending me the signal I was protected, and it calmed me for a few hours.

My thoughts galloped and raced through multiple scenarios as we got closer to Minneapolis. I pictured a loud and raucous hero's welcome as our bus pulled into our own high school parking lot. Prepared for the surprise, when we arrived at two a.m. to a desolate and empty lot except for our own cars, I cried uncontrollably. Not only was I no one's savior, but I knew I had to check into the hospital. Lauren drove us home.

I woke JD and asked him to drive me to Abbott, which was back on my insurance plan. Since it was the middle of the night, the freeway was clear. I looked out the window to see another deer, this time a doe, on the wrong side of the barrier fence. She, too, had an eerie calm to her, as if no harm would befall her so close to the highway. The sight of two deer in one night gave me an indelible image of strength and protection.

Unfortunately, it wasn't enough. I was unhinged and couldn't get a grip, so I checked into the locked ward. They gave me meds to sleep because I was agitated. The next day, Dr. Berger visited me on rounds.

"You're not okay, but there are a lot of sick people in the hospital. I'm worried it's not the best place for you right now," he said.

"What do you suggest?" I asked.

"I want you to recover at home, in your own bed." He signed the discharge.

"I never considered that. Didn't think it was an option," I said.

"You're half-baked. You need to rest. Call JD. You're going home." I threw the few belongings I'd brought into a bag and followed my psychiatrist right off the unit. It turned out there were secret, private passageways and doors physicians with keys used to come and go from the locked wards. In a matter of moments, I went from captive patient to freedom. The respect he showed me by sending me home restored my faith in the system and myself.

Since the job caused me and my family much more stress than the money could ever compensate for, I quit two months after returning to work. The scuttlebutt around the office was "she's faking" whatever mystery ailment caused me to miss three weeks of work. My breakdown was enough to allow me to see how unsafe some work environments are to disclose mental illness. My brother-in-law already knew. I never said a word to anyone else.

Chapter Twenty

Bonjour et Au Revoir

"*Parfait!*" said the first person I met as I deplaned at Charles de Gaulle. The customs agent flashed me a huge grin while my rusty translation skills made the switch from thinking he'd called me a whipped dessert to the status of the passport I'd just shown him. "Perfect," that's what he'd said, and I couldn't stop smiling.

We had been married twenty years, and JD planned the trip as the honeymoon we never took. I adored him for it. Paris had been a dream long before my first French class in ninth grade. The trip was an amazing gift, especially for me. I not only had studied the language but also felt a strong affinity for my French roots. My resilient bipolar grandmother, was, of course, French.

At my lowest weight since I started the psych meds, I proved to myself it was possible to lose girth while taking the medications. Dropping back to a size 6 was thrilling, albeit short-lived. By the time we left France, almost none of the clothes I'd packed still fit. I made a few other transatlantic newbie mistakes, like packing twelve pairs of pajamas, and lugging the giant bag around the country. We started and ended in Paris, spending two weeks touring the French countryside.

We walked along the Champs-Élysées, took a boat ride on the Seine, and blessed ourselves at Cathédrale Notre-Dame. Boarding a bus to tour Paris, I was eager to absorb the historical context. The ride was extensive and some of the passengers dozed, but I couldn't get enough. At one point, our guide grew quiet and I got an eerie feeling of familiarity, like I had been there before. The sensation developed into a horrible sense of dread for me. The tour leader, an Englishman, remained silent. Finally, half a mile later, he said, "Out of respect, we don't point it out, but we did pass the Pont de l'Alma tunnel, where the Princess of Wales was killed."

Sitting back in my seat, I felt my throat tighten, and my eyes welled with tears. Diana and I had been the same age, and I loved watching her come into her own. I had a dream the night she passed away. She came and spoke to me, telling me she'd wished she could've traded places with me. She would have loved to have been an anonymous housewife and mother to a bunch of kids, she told me. Despite my penchant for fantasy, the dream had seemed incredibly real.

I had no idea where we were relative to the city; I had simply intuited the significance when we passed the spot. It was a spiritual experience I will never forget. She was like a member of my own family. JD knew I was moved and drew me close, putting his arm around my shoulders.

I never thought of it while I was there, but when we returned to the States, I remembered the dream I had about Dr. Anderson while I was in his care ten years earlier, of being in Paris with my psychiatrist. It was far better in reality, with my actual husband, and it got me thinking and reassessing some of my daydreams.

Many had become what Garth Brooks correctly called "unanswered prayers" in one of his songs. I was riveted to my chair the first time I heard that tune. Mr. Brooks sang about praying for wishes that don't come to pass. The realization there's an excellent reason some prayers aren't answered made me feel fortunate when I figured it out for myself.

ꟸ

I had a dance I did with bipolar; I didn't speak of it outside of my support group, and in return, it left me alone. Facilitating the support group for people dealing with manic symptoms lasted for seven years. Leading the discussions supplemented my own intermittent therapy and allowed me to focus on other people rather than my own diagnosis. My involvement with the group ended in 2002. My ability to redirect people started to wane, and my heart was no longer in it. There were those who came into the meetings and eclipsed all other conversations due to active symptoms of the disorder. As a volunteer, I'd had enough. Looking back, I had alternatives, like finding a different location. I could have stayed on as a participant. I chose to move on instead. The hubris of feeling above the average bipolar survivor, because my symptoms were currently in remission, definitely played a part in my decision.

My cocktail of medications seemed to be effective, except for steady weight gain since the trip to France. I experienced what I imagined life was like for the unaffected. I dared to think of myself as "normal" for the time being. It had been a few years since I'd seen Dr. Malbec, and in the interim I'd attempted to establish a connection with two different female OB-GYNs. It didn't go well. Knowing he was out there and unavailable to me felt like I hadn't conquered my obsession. I hadn't.

Using my journal to bolster my decision, I convinced myself in 2002 I should go back to him. Sitting on the exam table and wearing another paper dress, drape, and a heavy cloak of denial, I waited. Bound and determined, I wanted to live without concessions to mental illness. I had decided no ill effects would befall me from a once-a-year office visit.

With the familiar quick double knock, he entered the room.

"Colleen, my dear, dear friend that I haven't seen in so long." With a huge smile, he stepped toward me, arms outstretched. Surprised, I offered my hand.

"A handshake won't cut it." He waved his hand, dismissing mine, and reached in to embrace me.

Here we go again, I thought. Per usual, I didn't object.

"You have no idea how happy it makes me to come into the office and see your name on my schedule," he said. Explanations as to why I came back seemed moot at this point, so I offered none.

"What have you been up to?" he said, as he began to palpate my right breast, checking for abnormalities.

"I've been writing a book."

He inquired what the book was about. We made small talk about women being better readers and buying the vast majority of books. He discussed his life, the fact he had also been to France, career accomplishments, family, and the size of his son's feet. This was a source of pride for some reason. I peeked at his own small black loafers and got the distinct impression it was an issue for him.

He put me back into the role of friend/therapist by lamenting how broke he had been, years ago, after he finished med school. He shared he'd never been to Europe until recently. Somehow, I wrenched the topic back to my illness and how I'd had a few relapses since we last spoke. Quickly, I placed the blame for the worst episode on my former psychiatrist. I relayed the story of how he had admitted being attracted to me, sought the opinion of his peers, and then retracted his confession.

"Shit," he said. "Even if it were true, that's so unethical. Get dressed. I'll be back."

His words seemed perplexing, even for him. It was obvious to me at that point he possessed limited insight into his own behavior. I wanted to take the conversation apart and digest it, but that would have to happen later. Even though I hurried to get dressed, he walked in too early as my sweater became bunched around my neck and I stood there in my bra and jeans. I quickly straightened the sweater as he walked toward me.

"When was your last mammogram? Let's go do it." He walked me down the hall toward their in-house radiology department. The technician was busy with another patient, so Malbec turned around quickly to face me. He told me when my lab tests would be back and looked down into my eyes with an unnecessarily sly grin. His body language, urgent and aggressive, felt intimate as he stood too close to me. His chest was so near mine I could feel his warmth.

The proximity seemed odd outside of the exam room. He was my dirty, secret crush. When he had walked in on me before I was dressed, I didn't object. But acting out in the halls seemed to throw the cloak of denial off and expose us both. He appeared immune and emboldened.

"I'll read your book. I'm in it. Hopefully disguised, reasonably," he said, as we stood in full view of other patients and staff. He wrapped his arms around my neck and pulled me closer to him.

"Make me six foot two and handsome," he said, and walked away.

I knew his attitude was wrong and unprofessional, yet in that moment I was his friend once again. Not a deluded mentally ill woman conjuring up a relationship that didn't exist. I hadn't imagined what he said and did. It legitimized him and the pseudosexual nature of our relationship.

After the mammogram, the technician raised a question about a spot she'd found. She suggested I shouldn't get dressed quite yet and instead ask the doctor what he thought. Still wearing the robe from the scan, I pulled a nurse aside in the hallway for assistance.

"Let me grab him," she said. The nurse explained to Malbec what I'd told her.

"You mean this?" He reached his finger through the opening in my robe and touched the top of my breast. He smiled, indicating to the nurse it was acceptable behavior. "It's nothing. Think of it as a freckle," he said.

The nurse made an angry *tsk* sound and looked at Malbec with a scowl. My lack of objection suddenly made me feel complicit and used. They walked away in different directions. I went back to the imaging room to get dressed, conflicted and confused. I had stepped into the sticky web he wove around me and volunteered to put my sense of propriety on a shelf in exchange for his attentions.

Amazingly, no obvious bipolar ill effects descended on me from that visit. No manic freak-outs materialized, and I rationalized reestablishing an annual visit to him would be okay and could do no harm. I decided I couldn't beat my obsession and wasn't willing to quit seeing him. I informed Dr. Berger after the appointment transpired and presented my case to continue in Dr. Malbec's care. Dr. Berger told me it was my choice to make.

What was not apparent were all the ways Al Malbec's presence in my life chipped away at the very self-esteem he was supposed to bolster. He called me his favorite patient. He said those words more than once. I actually believed him. Even in my most lucid moments, I felt used, yet ignored the feelings. If he truly respected me, his wife, his Hippocratic oath, none of this would have happened. If it really were just a case of transference, even sexualized transference, he could have referred me away.

He told me once that I wasn't the first patient to fall in love with him, nor would I be the last. He understood his patients' vulnerability by admitting this, while he reveled in their affections. What he didn't seem to grasp was how his ego came into play.

His own countertransference issues contributed to the mess I was feeling. Over the years, he told me explicitly he found me attractive. Women know, I knew, that was the case. I had no idea what to do with that information. Instead of repelled, it left me feeling muddled. For his own reasons and needs, he kept the door open on his end. This accomplished physician told me that I—someone who felt invisible most of her life—made his week simply by showing up in his office. Significantly younger than he and hopelessly naive, I was foolish to consider us friends. The ramifications for me were enormous: my marriage, family, self-image, and physical and emotional health were all on the line. He could claim, with apparent success, I was in it alone. The "relationship" was nothing of the sort. I had an attraction to him, and he was simply doing his job. His defense of himself as a self-proclaimed "supportive guy who takes care of women who aren't getting cared for at home" gave him free rein.

Al Malbec was an emotional cancer for me. I felt pulled to him in a primal way but dismissed it as fodder for my diary. The delusion was not that he had feelings for me. Most of the professional and personal advice givers I'd asked concurred he probably did. The bigger falsehood came in believing he'd admit them to me or himself.

But the most damaging, searing mistake was thinking contact with him didn't hurt me. It did. My saving grace was that it happened only once a year. The impression he singled me out in his world of women definitely made me feel special. But the sexualized nature of our relationship and the power vacuum it created for me didn't begin with Dr. Malbec.

I learned at a very early age men found me attractive. And that it was my fault. Except I had no words to that effect. It was second nature to me. I hated it and felt powerless because of it. In a different context, I heard the expression "Introduce a fish to water," and it opened my eyes. A fish lives surrounded by water all her life. In order to grasp the concept of the liquid environment, she must first understand her world is not like everyone else's. This was an enormous step for me.

The sexualized authority figure concept didn't come to me in one fell swoop. It took many years to realize the beliefs I had about myself, my sexual allure, its origins, and ramifications were false. I internalized the blame for men being attracted to me before I had any clue what that meant.

Dr. Anderson pointed out how the stories I conveyed about my dad confirmed my upbringing was tainted. I can still hear the clicking of Dad's ankles as he raced upstairs to slap us. The sound sent terror tremors to my stomach.

I remember being very confused by the fact my protector and guardian would hit us at night. It was never spoken of during the day. Neither of my parents mentioned the spankings, my sister tried to convince me we deserved them, and I had nowhere to take my feelings or objections.

My dad ruled the house with an iron fist. He was not to be challenged. Dr. Anderson did me a favor by explaining how my dad's actions and attitudes appeared to convey he had sexual feelings, conscious or not, toward me.

Dr. Anderson understood the mythology of my father as the all-powerful king of the family. Without a full picture of how all of it fit together, I was left seeking the attentions of the powerful. In this case, that was Malbec.

There were misplaced, crisscrossed, sexual urges around me my whole life. Wrong, but unfortunately, familiar. My almost instinctual attraction to Dr. Malbec stemmed from my sixth sense about his own boundary issues. He had an inability to separate his need to be adored from whatever attention he should receive from his patients. He presented himself as a sexualized authority figure, and I wanted to be in his sphere. It was all I wanted.

ꟸ ꟸ

October the following year, 2003, brought a return to Malbec's office. He was a hobby for me, while I no longer registered on his attention meter. I didn't mention the visit to anyone, even my husband. It embarrassed me that I continued to see Malbec when all signs pointed to moving on. He was part of the past, a crutch and a symbol of what never was.

That fall I reconnected with an old friend at a party. Through conversation, I discovered she knew Malbec well, they had worked together, so I asked her to meet for dinner. Over the course of the meal, she filled me in on what she knew of him. It was her opinion he did not hold women in high regard. When I mentioned I needed background for a book, she perked up.

"Someone should say something about him. I'm telling you, women will come out of the woodwork." She looked me in the eye. "He's got a reputation of being difficult to work with. What you picked up from the nurses not liking him at your delivery was spot on."

We discussed some of his frat-boy sexual exploits he'd shared with a fellow male physician in the operating room during surgery. Nurses listening in were either ignored or expected to abide by the rule: "What happens in the OR stays in the OR." The stories made both of us sick.

My friend questioned what I possibly saw in him that made me attracted to him or want to put my marriage in jeopardy. In my entire relationship with Malbec, no one had put it quite that succinctly. I told her he was charming, and it made me feel special. As we wrapped up the conversation, she left me with one last observation.

"He's known for that type of behavior toward many of his patients. I hate to be the one to burst your bubble, but you weren't singled out or special."

We hugged and she made me promise to write my truth. She assured me I'd be doing a service for many women who felt the way I did yet perceived themselves to be alone and voiceless. Her validation empowered me . . . until I got back to my car.

Once I was by myself, shame covered me in a blanket of despair. I had brought all of this on myself. I shook in my seat, complicit in the knowledge I willingly went back to him for reasons I couldn't readily explain. I couldn't answer the "why" questions without looking like some sort of addict. My friend had pounded the silver stake into the beast that was Malbec. It was up to me to leave it there and let the relationship wither or pull it out and deny what she had revealed to me.

As I drove home, my thoughts spun wildly. It took all my faculties to stay in my lane and keep my speed steady. I never questioned the veracity of her viewpoints. In my heart I knew she told the truth I refused to see. She filled in a lot of gaps in my vantage point, which was helpful and yet surprising, since I thought I knew a lot about him.

My decision to return was a year away.

ꕥ

Enough time had passed, and the revelations I'd discovered from my friend were no longer top of mind. In the fall of 2004, I went back to Al Malbec for another annual exam. It was a toss-up which man would show up for the appointment—the friendly, "so happy to see you" guy or the total dud who couldn't be bothered.

I wriggled onto the tissue paper atop the exam table in anticipation of his big entrance. I adjusted the blue paper dress over my nakedness and waited. He walked into the room, and I could immediately tell by his lack of enthusiasm which doctor he was.

He appeared haggard, tired, and older. The eyes I'd memorized as dancing and playful were now reddened, the crow's feet more pronounced. For the first time in seventeen years, I noticed his breath. It smelled stale and repugnant.

We chatted about our kids, and I told him we had built a new house. The energy between us felt listless. He continued the bland conversation and had begun the breast exam when we heard a knock on the door.

"Dr. Malbec here!" he said loudly and with authority. I reflexively covered myself. A middle-aged nurse entered, undeterred by his tone, and asked the doctor what I considered to be a nonurgent question. I shot him a look to convey my irritation. Her invasion of my privacy felt like a bigger violation than any I'd experienced from him. He apologized, yet the carelessness of the staff seemed to be a reflection of the culture in his office. *So what if you're naked? There are naked women in here all day, every day, and we don't respect them enough to notice.*

As I settled myself on the table, he got frustrated I wasn't near enough for the exam. He picked me up by both knees and pulled my crotch into the light, which was right in his face. Since I'd known him, I'd never been treated like that. He mentioned my uterus seemed slightly swollen, but nothing unusual.

He asked about the house we'd built and my new job as a realtor. It was clearly just another day at the office for him. I got dressed and he returned. Anticipating this appointment for months, I was disquieted by how badly it went. My history with him as a quasi friend made me think maybe he'd been having a bad day. I have no other rationale for what I did next.

"Do you have any questions?" he said.

As I formulated my response, time seemed to freeze. A debate flared in my head about wading into the whole sex thing again. If I brought up the intimate relationship with my husband, it might set off some signals I didn't want to send. I was still having issues, though, and I had legitimate questions. Regardless of the rest of the weirdness I'd experienced with him, he was my physician. If he played it straight, I would get some needed information. I decided to take the risk.

"I'm still having difficulty with sexual response," I began, trying to be as clinical as possible. "I need to rule out anything physical, you know, anatomical." The words came out in a jumble, and I regretted them as they were spoken. Everything about the day was wrong, off and disjointed.

He folded his arms and sighed. "It's probably the drugs you take, because your physical exam shows adequate vaginal moisture and there are no health issues." Then he thought for a moment. "You know, ninety-five percent of women complain about this. Frankly, most women's difficulty with orgasm is from the neck up, not the waist down."

Shock, revulsion, anger, and shame coursed through me, yet I remained mute. Such a ridiculously dismissive and disrespectful comment demanded a response. I put my most personal, closely held secret in his hands, once again, and he slapped me with it. He kept talking along the same lines, and I stopped listening. He folded up my chart and walked me out. He put his hand between my shoulders and rubbed my neck.

"Have fun decorating your house, Colleen," he said. It sounded peculiar to hear him use my name. As he walked away, he said, "See you next year."

"Like hell," I responded under my breath. With an almost audible *plink*, the bubble around him finally popped. All those years I'd dreamed, imagined, hoped, and fantasized we'd take what I'd perceived as a mutual attraction to fruition. In reality, he knew little about me.

The burning ardor I'd felt for this jerk chilled, replaced with cold disgust. The only thing smoldering in me now were the embers of my long-forgotten self-respect. It took longer than I'd ever imagined to walk away. And I did.

If I'd allowed myself to hear what he really thought about women, I would have realized his disdain. The fact he thought my idea of fun involved something as stereotypical as decorating finally broke me. That appointment unshackled me from my obsession. I didn't have the satisfaction of telling him off or explaining my absence. I simply never saw him again.

CHAPTER TWENTY-ONE

A New Start

A job with a home builder started the following winter, in 2005, and allowed me to pay for some college tuition for the kids. I retired our second minivan and traded up to a nice sedan. But the market for new homes took a nosedive in 2007, and working weekends lost its appeal, especially since I was no longer making any money. Depression descended on me personally, as well as on the US economy. I couldn't ask for any accommodations in my work hours because I chose not to disclose my illness.

Confiding in my boss on an out-of-town trip, I described very briefly my emotional entanglement with Dr. Malbec. The reason it was germane? It turned out she had been his patient at one time too. She shared she had lots of clients who used to get gussied up to go to their annuals because they "loved their Dr. Malbec." More proof, as if I needed it, I was far from the only one.

The depression got worse and, unable to sell enough houses to keep the tradespeople busy, I quit the real estate business, choosing instead to do volunteer hospitality at a small private hospice. The pressure to perform in the sales world had gotten to me, whereas making dinners for patients and their families was easy work, and it soothed my soul. My favorite moment was when a man hit his call button for help and the nurse asked me to check on him because everyone else was busy. I walked in to see tangled wires on his chest, which I mistook for something cardiac. "I don't think I can help you; I'm just a volunteer," I told him.

"Well, JV, this is a Walkman." We both laughed. I straightened out the mess and helped him put his headphones to his ears. He died the next day. I considered it an honor and a privilege to be with people at such a sacred time of their life. I stayed at my position for a year.

Feeling no rush, I took a couple of years after leaving Malbec before deciding to find a new doctor. Unlike the olden days of throwing a dart at the Yellow Pages, I began my search online. I read bios and reviews, and found someone not far from my house. I made an appointment.

Dr. Eric Heegaard walked into the room, shook my hand, and we talked. I told him I was a former patient of Dr. Malbec.

"I'm sorry," he said, with genuine empathy.

With two words, it was understood. No further discussion was necessary.

Thus began a fantastic, respectful, professional relationship. I voluntarily explained I had a long, on-again, off-again connection to Dr. Malbec and yet after all those years, never got my basic need for information met. We had an adult, candid conversation about female sexual response, which ended with a prescription and a solution Malbec had never even considered. My lifelong issue resolved in a few weeks.

During my initial appointment, Dr. Heegaard performed a physical exam, explained everything he was doing, and gave me some different, alarming news.

"How long have you had fibroids?" he said.

I thought he had me confused with someone else. "Me? Never."

"Well, you have a very large fibroid mass in your uterus. We need to do an ultrasound. Do you have time today?"

He was right. The previously undetected benign tumor had been growing for probably ten years, he told me. It was the size of a twenty-week fetus. A small basketball, he said. My first thought was of all the times I'd seen Malbec and he'd missed it completely, dismissing it as "a little swollen." After discussing my options, I decided to have Dr. Heegaard perform a subtotal hysterectomy.

I had no misgivings about the surgery, yet I had an irrational fear of running into Malbec at the hospital. The night before the procedure, I slipped into a mild manic episode. The dread of being confronted by my former doctor consumed me. I wasn't fully delusional, but I remember very little of the hospital stay. My brain was in overdrive and I fought sleep. Dr. Heegaard gave me Ambien and while I was sound asleep, I made an appointment to see Dr. Berger. When I failed to attend the appointment and received the no-show bill two weeks later, it took some detective work on my part to realize what I'd done. That was the end of Ambien for me.

My surgically removed uterus resulted in lots of cards, gifts, flowers, and sympathy. I couldn't help but notice the juxtaposition to the response people had when I needed psychiatric care. For the initial hospitalization people had rallied around me. After that, I sensed a compassion fatigue. Most of it was probably following my lead. Landing in the locked ward felt more like a failure to stay well than a time to collect congratulations for knowing to seek help. Feeling manic during a medical recovery was a complication I chose to keep within my immediate family.

The surgery required an abdominal incision because of the tumor's size. This made for a longer, more painful recovery for which I cursed Malbec and all the years I'd wasted mooning over him.

ꟸ ꟹ

In January of 2009, I entered an echelon of being that thoroughly took my breath away. I became a grandmother. Lauren delivered a son, Kyle, and all of us were bestowed new titles. So much had been written about parenting; earning the designation of grandparent was completely different in perspective and not nearly as accessible. It didn't seem to be described often enough.

I'd met a few grandparents in my life, but I'd never discussed with them how it felt to become one. Neither my own paternal grandmother nor my mother seemed to enjoy the role, and my other grandma, Evelyn, died when I was six. I loved my new status. It didn't need training to do; the skills were already there. With the elder wisdom also came a certain degree of authority not bestowed by age alone. I qualified as an expert for the first time in my life. It was, in a word, wonderful.

JD and I babysat as a couple, something I couldn't have imagined years earlier. We both adored little Kyle. We were five years into living in our new house, and Will was away at school. Sophie had graduated from college and was living in Chicago. All the kids were out of the house, I was not employed, and the timing felt perfect.

※

The next month, one of our neighbors asked us if we were interested in an investment opportunity. I was reticent and leery, but JD thought we should check it out. The neighbor picked us up. The men rode in the front seat while I sat behind. Our neighbor began to describe how the investment worked, but I wasn't convinced it made sense.

"It's like at the grocery store. Diversifying is not buying all produce or frozen food. You have to mix it up." Despite the inane analogy, I didn't jump on board. The man turned to my husband and said, "You have to put it in terms they understand." Then he smiled, figuring he knew so much about stocks and women.

If it wouldn't have caused me harm, I would have thrown open the car door and leapt. That condescending weasel wasn't to be trusted with any of my money decisions. As it was, he introduced us to an investment guru in the southern suburbs of the Twin Cities. Our neighbor had already invested heavily and was eager to share the idea. I found no compelling reason to give this supposed expert twenty-five cents and found the entire experience distasteful. JD, impressed with the investor's stated rate of return and track record, wrote him a small check to open an account. I remained skeptical.

In February, the Ponzi scheme made the news. The investor was indeed nothing more than a con artist, and his other victims had lost millions. JD had given him money based on the fraudster's falsified documents, and it was gone.

Trying to minimize the financial impact on us was impossible. The futility of "I told you so" did no good for me to assert. JD not only lost our investment but was shocked and embarrassed he hadn't seen it coming. The seismic effect of the loss caused distrust between us. Instead of rallying together against the common enemies who caused the fiasco, our relationship splintered.

Nine years had passed since my last hospitalization, and I thought of myself as impervious. The financial disaster proved too much for my brain. I stayed up until three a.m. reading everything I could get ahold of online regarding "How to tell if your spouse is cheating." My paranoia took over and eclipsed any version of reality. We had a miserable weekend full of vicious accusations and angry denials. Monday I threw in the towel.

I phoned Dr. Berger and told him I needed to be admitted. I was terrified thinking of going back after the experiences I'd had. Add to that the feeling of utter defeat and failure. Our investment was gone, our marriage trust was in tatters, and I convinced myself it was only a matter of time until JD admitted his infidelity.

Marni agreed to drive me to the hospital. The noise-abatement walls along I-35W rolled past my window. We didn't speak because I feared what I'd say about her dad. In a strange sensation, it felt like I had to budget what was left of my lucidity. I knew as we got closer to the hospital I'd soon be reduced to sitting on a bed and staring at the wall. My world closed in until nothing else fit in my brain except getting away. I could no longer comprehend loss of any type. It wasn't a blackout; I responded to the medical staff in the emergency room and answered their questions. Due to Dr. Berger no longer seeing patients in the hospital as part of his practice, I was assigned to a temporary psychiatrist and a bed on Station 48.

The patients there did not make eye contact with me and weren't responsive to psychotherapy or occupational therapy. It felt more like a human warehouse with vinyl furniture and constant television. Long gone was the environment I'd first walked into twenty years earlier. A lot of the programs were gone, and the pool had been shut down. I wasn't well, and Station 48 threatened what little sanity I had left. Within hours, I transferred to a less restrictive, but still locked, Station 39.

The first order of business was to change into suitable clothing. I was long a fan of medical dramas, so the scrubs they offered me were a personal thrill and bucket-list accomplishment. The clothes I wore from home were taken. The unmarked scrubs were comfortable and gave me a sense of belonging, a oneness with the staff.

I met the doctor assigned to me. She happened to be a friend of Dr. Berger's, which helped tremendously with my general trust issues. I accepted the strong sedatives she prescribed and rested for the first time in over a week.

Despite the sedatives, I awoke the next morning at five forty-five. Restless, I sat in the community room, alone. On The Unit it felt cool, to the point of being cold, no matter what the temperature outside. The common-area lights weren't allowed on until seven a.m.

I had misplaced my glasses the night before. Completely unaware I could enlist a staff member to help me find them, I thumbed through a worn, outdated magazine held close to my face. I stared at the door, hoping the breakfast trays would arrive early to give me something to do. The door opened.

Even though I could barely see, I knew by his gait the man with the raincoat: my husband. He looked straight ahead carrying a brown paper grocery bag. I could see him smile at the nurse as he handed over the bag. Still angry with him, both for the real and imaginary deeds he had perpetrated, I didn't get up. I waited for him to see me and come talk to me. He turned his back to me and, without a glance, walked right off The Unit and out to the heavy locked door. A staff member buzzed him through, and he was gone.

My heart crushed inside my chest. He either hadn't seen me or chose to walk right past me. What if that was what my future looked like? Stripped of all I held dear because I was incarcerated in a place like this and unable to function. My actions had consequences, and maybe my long-suffering husband had had enough.

Whether the snub was intentional or not, the resulting effect caused me to reflect.

There were no magic pills for mentally ill patients like me to take in the hospital. Most of the medications were to control behavior, and that wasn't my issue. There were only sleeping meds and the same drugs I took when I was at home. Getting out of the hospital and regaining mental sobriety happened within brief spurts of time. This was one of those moments. I had an epiphany: I wasn't a self-righteous, accusatory madwoman anymore. It felt like black was becoming a very dark gray. The process of healing had begun, thanks to the realization my husband may have finally run out of patience with me.

Mercifully, the lights in the hallway came on. The carts carrying the trays with brown plastic covers came rumbling through the same door my husband had exited earlier. The slightest glimmer of something resembling normalcy resonated in my head, and I felt the tide turn toward trying to get better.

I attended the obligatory therapy and Group sessions for the rest of that day and three more. I mostly guessed at the responses I offered in Group. This earned me the privilege of a day pass. I could go home to test how well I handled it, as long as I promised to sleep in the hospital. I'd made a lot of progress in realizing the distrust of my husband as one of the symptoms of mania. We arranged to have JD pick me up after lunch the next day.

As logic returned to my skill set, I relearned JD was trustworthy. I made the jump back relatively quickly while no one around me, including my husband and the staff, had the benefit of seeing inside my head. Rational thoughts seemed to return one at a time, like flipping on spent circuit breakers.

Every hour that passed seemed to help thin the veil shrouding my sanity. I likened it to warming up someone suffering from hypothermia. It had to be done slowly, not by throwing the person into hot water. My thinking cleared up regarding JD. The realization my altered mind had tarnished him with thoroughly untrue accusations made me remorseful and sad. I had to fight the crescendoing anxious feelings I would never be completely free of the hospital. The paranoia I might unintentionally do something to jeopardize my release hung over me.

That evening I sat in the community room again; this time it was teeming with patients. I sat alone at a table, with tears streaming down my face. They were angry, self-pitying rivers I didn't care to hold back. A painful but necessary step in leaving madness behind. One of the patients approached me with a conspiratorial whisper.

"Same thing happened to me," he said.

I ignored him and pumped out more saline from my swollen eyes.

"You just figured out you're not God after all, didn't you?"

Stunned, I didn't even have my own words for it, yet he'd captured the emotion exactly. A mystical, deity-like sureness had left me moments before, leaving behind the realization I was all too human. And a sick one at that.

"How did you know?" I asked with a quavering voice.

He went on to explain how God came and went in this place. There were times he could tangibly feel an amazing strength and power within himself. The problem was, when it left, and it always did, he needed to be in a safe place.

"I've felt what you're feeling," he said. "It's lonely. And shitty. But it's kind of a relief." Then he shuffled away.

The moment careened me toward my version of normal. I'd also heard patients refer to it as a "divine exorcism." I got rapidly better after that. The nurses said the drugs were kicking in, but I contended in my mind, there was space for both explanations. And it was not to be confused with being abandoned by a higher power.

The feeling of omnipotence, God-like and fearless, had to leave in order to assume my humanity.

On Sunday, the patients and staff were busy planning an Oscars party for that night. There would be popcorn and candy, and we would all watch together. As part of my release agreement, I had to make it back for the event. I wanted to run far from that place and never return, but I did as I was told.

JD picked me up after lunch. It wasn't real until I got outside the hospital. The sun and breeze on my face made freedom intoxicating. Even the feeling of riding in a car felt unfamiliar but equally wonderful. When I got home, I took a nap in my soft sheets and sank into the cushiony mattress. I soaked in all the smells and scents of my big house in the suburbs. After we'd eaten an early, light dinner, the news came on about the upcoming Oscars telecast, reminding me I had to go back. I'd never related more to Cinderella and her pumpkin.

When we got back to the hospital, we were met at the door of The Unit, and JD had to leave. He said he'd be back the next day to bring me home. I refused to shed any more tears, fearful it would be interpreted as instability. I kissed him goodbye and went to the community room for the last time.

I took my seat near the television. I crunched on a bowl of cooled popcorn while my fellow patients dwindled in number and lost interest, returning to their rooms. As I watched the parade of presenters and recipients, I had one last grandiose thought. I saw Simon Beaufoy win Best Adapted Screenplay for *Slumdog Millionaire*. I imagined myself in the future, when I would accept my own Oscar for the same award, and I would thank all the folks in community rooms everywhere. I would tell the world how far I'd come and quote Winston Churchill: "*Never* yield to force; *never* yield to the apparently overwhelming might of the enemy." Especially the enemy within your own mind.

Chapter Twenty-Two

Gradual Decline

In 2009, the brain trust in charge of a huge clinic in the Twin Cities area fired most of their mental health providers. These were busy doctors with hundreds, if not thousands, of patients. They provided too much care, supposedly. Time spent per patient in relation to revenue didn't add up to big-enough profits, based on insurance reimbursements. They let the entire department go, including the doctors, and shuttered their offices.

One of those physicians was Dr. Berger. He decided to take early retirement, so following him to another clinic was not an option. Dr. Berger and I had worked together for fourteen years, and the news devastated me. It felt like someone kicked over an anthill, leaving many semi-orderly lives in chaos. The firings affected a lot of the patients I had known in the support group; we were all in the same boat.

Fortunately, our financial picture had rebounded after the swindle fiasco, and we purchased a lake cabin. The tranquil place Up North transformed both our marriage and my state of mind. I'd conjured up a cabin purchase for the protagonist in my novel years earlier yet never believed it could become a reality in our lifetimes. The drive to get there provided a perfect opportunity for uninterrupted conversation. We spent a comfortable number of weekends entertaining friends and family, while the majority of the time we were alone in the woods. The bucolic setting soothed my psyche and bestowed on us a welcome chance to relax.

Refreshed by the cabin acquisition, I went in search of a new doctor. Since my last trip to the hospital, I'd been working with a therapist named Sara Biewen, and we were still getting to know each other's style. Sara was one part of the care team equation and became a valuable asset, while the position of psychiatrist cycled from bad to worse.

The first doctor I hired to replace Dr. Berger looked at me like a deer in headlights when manic symptoms returned. I knew we weren't a good match early on, but her inability to handle even a small health crisis meant we were completely through and I got up and walked out of the session. She chased me to the elevator, telling me I wasn't well. *No shit, Sherlock*, I thought. I checked myself into the hospital later that night. We had to cancel a big Memorial Day gathering at the lake, and the degree of that disappointment weighed heavily on me.

I was in for three days when they offered a new option: partial treatment. This was for patients who were sick enough to need treatment to stabilize, but not ill enough to be in residence in a hospital. It required me to go to the hospital every weekday from nine a.m. to three p.m., and I could sleep in my own bed. By the end of the week, I was home and looking for yet another new doctor.

I considered myself near the top of the pyramid for mental health consumers, based on the resources at my disposal. Most of the fellow patients I'd encountered on my journey had it worse. Mental illness cast its shadow over all socioeconomic strata, and I was conscious of my privilege and how it informed my choices. My limited options for psychiatrists still surprised me, and I became acutely aware of a desperate shortage of decent practitioners.

ꕥ

During this shift between doctors, Marni told us she was having a difficult time in her life. I could trace her depression to the days before she started elementary school, yet the last few years proved even more painful. Suffering from gender dysphoria, she informed us of her identification as male. For the family, the transition seemed abrupt, but for Lucas, as he is now known, it was the culmination of changing a lifetime of unhappiness.

I always said, "How could those parents be caught off guard? How could they not know?" Then it happened in my family. What I knew for sure: my child had been miserable for a long while. The reasons could always be explained away as circumstantial: school, friends, job. Everything could heal with a new one. But a new identity? I wanted to be supportive. My fear for him took center stage.

The family processed Lucas's transition each in our own way. Grief played a huge part. Marni ceased to exist, and we mourned her. Lucas was ready to move on with his life. Pronouns switched and mistakes were made, but there was no retreating or going back possible. Lucas modeled courage and bravery for all of us, but I stumbled. Selfishly, I searched Lucas's life for what I might have done wrong. Taking the blame for being a poor mother and not realizing what the issues were earlier, I internalized the pain of losing Marni and made the circumstances surrounding Lucas's transition about me.

Four months later, Sara, my therapist, noticed changes in my behavior. I became unusually irritable, staying up late, ruminating, and having trouble concentrating. She insisted I check in with my latest doctor. The clinic had no availability or even telephone access over the weekend. By Monday, I had escalated past hypomania to a full-blown manic state.

By the time I got to the clinic, it had taken so long to get in, my anger boiled just below the surface. It was torturous waiting to be seen.

"So, how are you feeling?" Dr. Worthless said in the hallway, oblivious to my mood.

"Not. Well. This is a shitty time to find out this clinic has no after-hours or weekend care. Now I need a hospital bed. Do you think you can manage that? I need to grab lunch. Call me when you find something."

He smiled mirthlessly, gave a note to the receptionist, and went back to his office. I turned around and left.

My sisters and mom had accompanied me to the appointment, thinking they'd bring me to the hospital afterward. I insisted I was okay enough to have lunch out, but Pat knew better. I was a powder keg and ready to blow up at anybody who looked at me sideways. We went home.

A nurse called that afternoon and told me, "I tried to do you a favor, but there are no available beds anywhere. You could try the emergency room. Goodbye." My family members were astonished. I said, "Welcome to what most people deal with in the mental-illness realm." I called Sara again, and she got me back into the partial program, averting a worsening meltdown.

The therapists and doctors at the hospital were discouraged to see me back there. It's not a place you want to have everybody know your name, like Norm from *Cheers*. In group therapy, we had to share why we were there. I told the hospital therapist and my fellow patients about Lucas. Usually, people join in with their own stories of a relatable experience. The room fell silent.

The therapist looked vaguely familiar. I searched my memory, then it dawned on me. She had done the family therapy with my parents and siblings twenty-three years earlier. That night, I dug up my photocopies of her handwritten notes of the session, all those years earlier, and brought them to show her. I don't know what surprised her more, the fact I recognized her in my compromised state or that I saved copies of my hospital records.

I absentmindedly mentioned to the group participants I was leaving for my cabin for the weekend when Friday came. This sent one of the patients into a tirade because she didn't have her own cabin. I felt foolish for being insensitive and ridiculously pampered. I also knew my time there was finished. We drove away and, like every other time, acted like it never happened.

Chapter Twenty-Three

Testing the Net

A letter arrived shortly after my release from the partial program. Dr. Berger had returned to psychiatry as a solo practitioner. The three years I'd spent out of his care had been miserable. I quickly signed on as his patient again. Life was mercifully uneventful for the next two years as I spent my time searching for a suitable smaller home for my husband and me. In June 2014 we downsized to a townhome in the same suburb.

When school started that fall, I watched my grandson, Kyle, get off the kindergarten bus every day for a week, then he'd be with his dad for a week. My life followed a structured plan. My own marriage was solid, and we spent most weekends relaxing at the lake. I had both a core group of friends and those I saw a little less often. Living went from chaotic struggles to a manageable existence. Bursting with hubris, and taking full credit for my emotional sobriety, I made the decision the mood-stabilizing meds were a bother and not necessary with all the support systems I had in place.

I titrated the doses down, secretly and on an experimental basis, until I wasn't taking them at all. Five months elapsed and predictably, the outer edges of my rock-solid marriage started to fray. Trust gave way as the days grew darker and colder. I made no connection that the lack of chemical stabilizers was responsible for my mood changes. Instead, I again was visited by the specter of distrust and paranoia. I insisted we begin marriage counseling.

Exasperated and confused, JD agreed. He had no idea my suspicions and wariness were fueled by the suspension of the medications. He was certain that delving into our relationship would not reveal any wrongdoing on his part, and he figured learning to communicate more effectively would only improve the situation. We learned some techniques, like becoming curious about each other instead of complacent. JD seemed to look forward to the sessions because therapy was a relatively new world for him. Our previous marriage-therapy sessions had been short-lived. I'd been in counseling on and off for over twenty-five years, so I soon tired of it.

In an erratic trajectory, my moods grew volatile. Only in retrospect could I see the low-grade irritability simmering under the surface of most conversations. Desperate to believe we, which meant mostly me, had turned a corner, I insisted we find a new wedding ring set to celebrate our now-healed relationship. My original wedding band didn't fit, and I still had a bee in my bonnet about not getting an engagement ring. We did a lot of shopping, but nothing spoke to me.

Finally, we found our way to a beautiful jewelry store that had a combination of estate and new rings. I saw a traditional three-stone engagement ring with a remarkable center diamond. It was previously owned, but the proprietor cleverly "couldn't remember" the circumstances or the story behind the ring. It could have been a divorce, a broken engagement, or simply an upgrade opportunity for the woman who used to wear it. I decided to adopt the ring and rewrite its history, just like I was trying to repackage my marriage. We picked out a thin platinum wedding band to match so I'd have a whole new set. The engagement ring needed resizing and would be ready in a few days.

I awoke at the cabin on a sparkling Saturday in May. JD was on bended knee, holding a beautifully wrapped jewelry box with a big bow. He asked me to marry him, not in a do-over, but for the first time. Thirty-four years earlier, we had skipped over the formality. Truly moved and thrilled by our fresh start, I wanted to stay in that moment forever. We made plans to take a trip to Martha's Vineyard in the fall.

If I could have, I would have wrapped a cocoon around us to shield us from any further threats to our happiness. I tried with all my might to be a helpful partner, a solid contributor to the union, but I possessed no such powers. In fact, my fragile stability couldn't withstand even the slightest hint of stress.

My father, a thirty-five-year cancer survivor, experienced a new onset of the disease. My mom could no longer drive, so she enlisted me as their driver to take them to clinic and chemotherapy appointments.

The relationship with my dad remained outwardly cordial while I seethed inside with the frequent contact. The stress of pretending I wasn't resentful took a major toll on my emotional well-being. I was a giving person. I had no problem being a caregiver, especially since he was sick. It was the dynamic of our relationship. He could only relate to me by telling me what to do: which lane to travel in, where to park, which cars to pass.

When we got to the clinic, he would point out which direction to push his wheelchair and loudly comment about the appearance of other patients. I muzzled myself from interacting with him or telling him to knock it off. The cumulative effect of not only stuffing my irritation in the present but bristling around him for years in the past made the situation untenable.

I didn't get along with my father for a variety of reasons. He displayed a palpable lack of respect for women yet, in my lifetime, had never been challenged on that point. It was the unwritten, unspoken rules in my family that chafed my psyche: Thou shall not question the provider, on anything. Ultimate respect and honor are to be bestowed on the father regardless of his behavior. Dad has the right to belittle, criticize, or complain about the rest of the family, but it never flows the other way publicly.

When I put myself in close proximity to my dad, it provided more opportunities to butt up against his policies of lashing out at people. It got to the point where I was either triggered in the present or reminded of past incursions, yet I continued to pretend we got along.

The debacle years earlier, when I tried to broach the subject of our twisted sexualized relationship, had ended in me apologizing, dropping the topic, and internalizing the resentment. Far from resolving it, I tried to push the conflict down. It was akin to trying to grasp an air bubble and keep it underwater.

Regardless of the discord with my dad, my fifty-something self still yearned to be in his favor. I witnessed a much easier relationship between my other siblings and him. My inner child still got in line for whatever crumbs of attention would drop my way. That was the rationale behind the rides to the clinic. Despite all the turmoil, a part of me still sought his love.

CHAPTER TWENTY-FOUR

The Unraveling

Traffic on I-94 coming home from the cabin stood still. It was late August in 2015, and we decided to take a detour in order to keep moving.

As the new landscape drifted past, I chose to use our newly acquired communication techniques to discuss some unexplored territory with my husband.

"Do you think it's true, what Dr. Anderson said about my dad after I got diagnosed?"

"What do you mean?" JD replied.

"He said it sounded like Dad had some creepy ideas about me, as a child. Now that I'm spending so much time with him, it bothers me. I've never gotten it out of my head."

"I have no idea," he said. "But then again, I can't picture anyone capable of that."

Many times before, both on therapy couches and in the privacy of my own journal, I'd pushed myself to try to remember actual instances of sexual abuse, yet I came up blank. Whether the lack of mood stabilizers, or the abrasive, continual exposure to my father finally opened the closed door, I'm not sure.

My husband and I drove in silence. I watched the farms and small towns roll past my window. The gears of my mind began to spin. Then I heard it inside my head. Like white noise or a constant hum, I remembered the sound from as far back as my mind could reach. It was the sound of dread.

I appeared to be looking out the window of the car, yet my mind went back in time. I was little, way before school age. A strange throbbing sensation, like a pulse, but faster, between my legs. I was confused and I didn't understand. Suddenly, like granite puzzle pieces shifting into place, it all made sense.

The feelings were my body reacting naturally as a child. Instantly I was flooded with the realization that two of the defining questions of my life were related phenomena. Why was I anorgasmic for so many years, and was I ever touched inappropriately as a child? The memory I'd just experienced proved to me the relationship of how the two had become jumbled together. Not only was I orgasmic as a child, but I must've learned to block out the association with genital stimulation. I was robbed of an instinctual, primal gift before I ever had the chance to experience it as a mature, willing participant.

"Don't move!" the voice said in my now clear memory. I responded to the sensations, and the perpetrator, my father, yelled at me. The connection between sexual response, shame, fear, degradation, and an eagerness to please had become a tangled mess for me before kindergarten age. Everything about the feelings was wrong, very wrong. I felt powerless, trapped, and afraid.

No clues materialized to place me in the time of day or in which room this occurred. Anger permeated the experience. My dad was mad at me for something. I had displeased him somehow. I wanted to be a good girl, worthy in his eyes, but I had no idea what was going on. I also knew this was not the first time. He had called it "the game." Then I was flooded with a memory that crystallized the recollections. The sense that never failed me when everything else was lost to madness. I remembered the smells.

I had a clear memory of the scent of my own genitals as a child and the association with shame, self-loathing, and feeling dirty. Such a horrific message he gave to a young female child.

The connection between my father and recovered memories of being molested as a little girl finally collided. I was certain now. There was no longer a need for him to validate the images, and no one else was there. With a shivering jolt, I came back to the present as an adult.

My body went hot, then icy cold. I shook violently as if to rid myself of the memories.

"Damn him to hell!" I shrieked.

"What?" JD was not privy to any of the recollections.

"It wasn't a dream or my imagination. It was real. I was abused by my own father!" My screams filled the car as it raced down the winding two-lane road.

"Shit. It's been my biggest fear my whole life that one day it would be true. I've figured it out. It's a freaking nightmare, JD!"

"I'm sorry," he said, without hesitation. "Do you want me to pull over?"

"No," I sobbed. "I want to go home."

"Oh crap," he said. "My car is downtown, and we have to pick it up. Are you okay to drive?"

I wiped my face with the palm of my hand. "Yeah. I think so. I will be by the time we get there."

JD pulled up to his downtown Minneapolis office tower forty-five minutes later and jumped out. I climbed over to take the wheel of my own SUV.

Navigating through the near-empty city streets, I headed west toward home. Beams of setting sunlight streamed at me and surrounded the vehicle. The God voice I heard first after Will's birth and many times later should be arriving any minute, I thought. Alone in my car with these revelations of abuse, I craved the voice again. It didn't come. Instead, I heard my own stifled wails as the tears flowed down my face for the little girl I pictured in my mind.

Although I was repulsed by the images of the actual abuse, what shocked me more were the feelings of relief. For decades, I'd questioned why I had such animosity toward my father, and despite years of therapy, the portal to the answer remained closed. Now the pieces made sense, and the ominous fear of the unknown could be replaced with the truth.

I gripped the steering wheel tighter to ground myself in the present. This time, I wasn't going to run off and tell anyone in my family. Imagining the repercussions of tossing a bomb into that group rallying around infirm Dad caused the first inklings of mania. The reprisals wouldn't be the worst of it. They would question my sanity and call me delusional. Fearing their lack of support, I knew to process my feelings away from the wolf pack.

JD and I arrived home around the same time and busied ourselves with unpacking my car.

"Do you want to talk about it?" he asked.

"Not now. Let's just get this stuff put away, then I need to get some thoughts on paper."

I'd been hacking away at my novel for years, and suddenly it was incredibly important to sketch an outline for a different book, based on what I now knew to be true. My pen flew over the page; anger erupted like molten lava. I hated the feeling of victimization. My father had stolen something from me before I was aware I owned it. Then gaslighted me by denying it back in 1995. Sleep, my most precious resource against mania, proved elusive that night.

Two days later I saw Sara for a regularly scheduled appointment. To her, the description of memories recalling sexual abuse seemed a natural, almost eventual, escalation from what I'd shared earlier about my relationship with my dad. Unaware of my medication experiment, she gave me feedback about the telling of my story. Sara observed that my thoughts seemed scattered and loose. She asked me to check in anytime if my mind deteriorated, and suggested I chart my moods to foretell a manic spike. I agreed, and left, the ominous clouds of mania already gathering.

I tried desperately to maintain a normal schedule while I tamped down not just the reconstituted memories but the consequences of telling. Sharing my revelations with Sara seemed to have stirred up my emotions rather than provide relief. One foot on the accelerator, ruminating, and the other pressing the brake, not telling my brothers and sisters, took its toll. I didn't fully comprehend how my tenuous situation was beginning to unravel, and in a combination of stubbornness and pride, chose not to reach out further to Sara for professional help.

My niece's baby shower had been on my calendar for weeks. On any given day, I could throw a party with aplomb. It happened to be something I did a lot and enjoyed. This one caught me flat-footed, yet I refused to make concessions or look to a helper. I stayed up the night before, searching the internet for pink punch recipes, hanging elaborate paper decorations, and setting out pink flatware. I planned a fancy dessert to impress the hell out of the guests and prove my mettle as a hostess, despite the jarring revelations.

The party took place the next evening, a blistering August Wednesday. No match for the twenty-five animated women milling around the kitchen, the air-conditioning failed to cool the house. Despite my last-minute rush the night before, I felt disorganized and couldn't manage the party.

After the gift opening, I sensed people were eager to leave. If I'd been on my toes, the dessert would have been chilling in the refrigerator, berries floating in peaks of airy cream and pressed against their trifle dish. By contrast, the strawberries weren't even sliced, the cake I'd made from scratch had yet to be torn into chunks, and the liquid in the carton should have been whipped into cream.

Finally, desperate, I begged my sister Maureen for help. I tossed her the handheld mixer and beaters, and she reluctantly accomplished the task. Maureen and my guests didn't care two bits about the treat. They were hot and restless. Nobody helped clean up or had taken any pictures. Devastated, I served the soupy dessert disaster. A few of my sisters insisted on gathering some of the other leftover food for Dad as a care package before they left. This annoyed me most of all, yet I couldn't tell them why.

The hosting debacle unmoored me. By the time the last guest left, I felt myself go away, mentally. I went into my home office to gather my thoughts. Finding none, I wrote in my journal about the flashbacks I was having and bombs of revelations about the abuse. The entries were all scrawled, lines skipped, words strangely misspelled.

Sleep didn't come easily for JD or me. The one-way mania train caused my thoughts to race. While I was restless and rolling on my side of the bed, JD could sense impending instability amid the insomnia. He insisted I take something to get me to sleep. He told me if I didn't, he'd stay up all night watching me sleep and doze off at work the next day. We both knew it was critical to force sleep because natural fatigue didn't exist for me when I was too far gone. JD would lie awake listening to my breathing. He told me he felt powerless, like watching me fall off a cliff. It was a lose-lose situation. I gulped down a sleep aid and fifty milligrams of the antipsychotic Seroquel. It was a light dose, but it caused me to miss Thursday altogether. I awakened at five in the evening on August 27, 2015, and found a long-awaited copy of Brené Brown's new book, *Rising Strong,* had been delivered to my doorstep.

My close friend Beth and I had been making plans to head to Chicago to see Brené at a book signing. I'd waited months on a list for the email to unlock our tickets to the event. Divine intervention, in the form of a computer glitch, had opened the tickets to the general public, instead of the wait list, and they sold out to strangers in minutes. In my manic state, I screamed at Brené (electronically) for allowing such a failure. A polite staff member sent a sincere apology email. If I'd gotten through to purchase the tickets and traveled to Chicago *again* while sick, I didn't want to imagine the consequences.

Instead, deeply disappointed and at home, I pretended to be well. The sleeping pill and antipsychotic cleared my thought processes for a few days. On Monday, JD and I attended a party to celebrate a small health victory for my father. Teri, Michelle, and Pat opened champagne and danced around Dad's wheelchair to honor him. I stood back, remaining still, unable to see him as anything but a child abuser. The contradiction in reactions between my sisters and me made a rent in the fabric of my brain. I didn't want to participate, yet I couldn't bring myself to stay away.

An entry in my journal on Wednesday began: STAR DATE SEPTEMBER 2, 2015. I wasn't a huge *Star Trek* fan, so it was completely out of character. Nothing positive could follow that, and it didn't.

Now completely manic, I phoned Dr. Berger later that day. In a calamitous turn of events, he either didn't get the message or didn't grasp the severity of the situation. He never returned my call.

Unlike during some of my other decompensations, I had an outward face of calm. It belied the fact I was utterly delusional. While JD made himself dinner, I packed a bag. The items I included made sense at the time: my new, highly prized copy of *Rising Strong,* photocopies of hospital records from 1989 that were irreplaceable and should never leave my office, a treasured journal from the same time, and my current journal. These items would be evidence when Dr. Malbec showed up at the hospital to take me away with him. Although I had written him off years earlier, the fantasy rekindled like a raging wall of water filling a dry riverbed.

I tried to remain calm. The effort was the equivalent of squeezing a balloon to make it shrink. The stress reappeared in other areas, even larger, pushing my psyche to the breaking point. At this point I was planning to run away with Malbec, listening to a Universal frequency where God communicated with me through songs on the radio, colors of flowers, or combinations of numbers. Everything I looked at referenced God. I couldn't take a nap or rest because I might miss something important.

At eight o'clock that night, I had one of my last linear thoughts. I decided if Malbec were to meet me as we telepathically planned, I needed to head to the hospital. JD got in the car and drove me, unaware of my ulterior motives. He figured he'd wait with me until I was admitted. I had no idea when Dr. Malbec would appear, so I convinced him I'd be okay in the emergency department until they took me upstairs. I would call him in the morning when I settled into my room. JD didn't like the idea, but he left me when I assured him I knew the procedure and would be fine.

Chapter Twenty-Five

The Last Time

Once I was alone, the descent into madness accelerated. I didn't need JD worrying or demanding answers. I'd asked him to leave to allow Dr. Malbec to come rescue me. I'd been wrong before, but this time he was really coming.

It felt odd to be alone, especially there, but necessary. I knew what to say, and I didn't want anyone to speak for me. They'd ask me a few questions, find me a bed, and in a day or two I'd be back home. The place smelled the same; disinfectants for the floors and isopropyl alcohol permeated the air from prepping all the injections.

I'd never seen this part of the emergency department. Where were all the people? I was left in a secluded hallway, but I knew they were watching me. It felt like a test. I'd show them they couldn't break me. I refused to throw a loony fit just because they were ignoring me. I could wait it out because I knew he was coming. Al was on his way.

"Colleen? Can you answer a few questions for me about why you're here?" The woman in scrubs sat down at the desk in the small room I'd been in for hours. Her face appeared pleasant and I decided to trust her. She had an empty plastic bag with her. I gave her the old journal, the one from June 1989. All my writing would prove to be prophetic and would explain who I was (God) and my peaceful mission.

We got through my full name, birth date, and address. This I did effortlessly.

"Can you tell me what brings you in here tonight?" she said.

"I've been having a lot of positive, happy thoughts. Really

wonderful stuff. And a lot of connectivity. And songs"— *I know these are messages from God*— "randomly play on the radio or in stores. My favorite number is twenty-two, and this is room twenty-two. Synchronicities like that don't happen by accident."

I measured my responses. I could fill her whole computer with what I knew, but I'd learned not to say too much. Just crazy enough was the goal.

"Anything else?" she asked.

"Yes. I have thoughts of grandeur and ideas of reference. And God won't stop talking to me. It got worse on Monday, August 24, 2018," I said proudly and specifically, unaware I'd said the wrong year.

It was coming, I could feel it. In fact, I didn't want to hold it back. *Shit, maybe this is why I decided to come back here. I need to tell somebody, and these people might be able to help me.* She let me continue, so I did. I liked the sound of her fingers as she clicked on the keyboard while I spoke. It made me feel important.

"I know what pressured speech is. I don't have that. I'm not grandstanding, like when you can't shut up. I have a call in to my psychiatrist, but he hasn't called me back. I tried to stabilize myself at home, but I can't sleep and I can't make the God stuff go away. I've had flashbacks about my other episodes. I was brought in here in an ambulance once."

I pulled up at this point. She had enough information to admit me, and it felt too scary to tell her everything. So I didn't mention Dr. Malbec was coming. Instead, I told her about my frustration at caring for dear old, sick Dad. How he always tried to control me, even though I pushed the wheelchair, and it drove me mad.

"I knew he was a child abuser. He abused me. I thought years of criticisms and belittling comments toward me were enough reason to resent him. But ten days ago, when my husband and I took a different way home from the lake, the images of abuse fell together like shards in a kaleidoscope." She didn't react or stop typing, so I continued. "I was very young, definitely not in school yet, but the flashes and visions I saw in my mind's eye were crystalized and real. I was concerned no one in my family would believe me because I was 'the crazy one' and it didn't happen to them."

I wanted to be admitted at that point, but it wasn't because I thought I was sick. I had to be at the hospital so Dr. Malbec would come to get me while my dad and JD could not.

That's how I did it. I revealed my abuse. I told her everything. Now it was in my chart. As it ended up, I skipped the part about Dr. Malbec because I was starting to realize there was a slight possibility I was mistaken about him still being into me and wanting to protect me. Time would tell, I thought.

The nurse wanted to know if I would sign an opt-out statement, which meant nobody would know I was in there. The hospital wouldn't even confirm whether I was a patient there, let alone in the locked mental unit. Most of my family never visited me there anyway, and I would be embarrassed if my friends found out. The news media might call too, I figured, so I signed it. If Kim Kardashian had a breakdown, that's what she would do.

I denied any suicidal or homicidal thoughts, which was easy because I had none. I also told them I didn't abuse chemicals or practice self-harm, which was also true. She collected my phone, purse, and the set of staff notes from my initial hospital stay. I brought them with me to prove I was God then, as I was now. My most prized possession was the Brené Brown book, but I couldn't concentrate enough to read it, so I handed it over with the rest of my stuff.

The nurse disappeared and I waited. I couldn't see a clock; I had no watch or phone. I also didn't have a window. I stepped out into the empty hall but was afraid to leave my room. I had no interest in escaping my open cage. Been there, done that. My mind sometimes went into Zen-like gears at times of severe stress. It was completely self-taught. I pushed down and away all my surface feelings, like wanting to scream at people. It felt more powerful to get really quiet.

A different young woman in scrubs came into my room. I noticed her credentials on her lanyard. She seemed to be a nurse and she carried a lot of keys. She also had a maroon set of scrubs, emblazoned with a large BH on each piece, for me. I quickly decoded the markings. It stood for Behavioral Health. Nobody would want to steal those, or wear them, for that matter. She watched me change into them to make sure I didn't bring anything dangerous onto The Unit. No pockets, no drawstrings. My athleisure outfit was crumpled into yet another plastic bag. I smiled because I couldn't believe it. They were finally admitting me, but my mouth was dry from nerves and my lips stuck to my teeth. Whatever the intentions of the blood-red, boldly lettered scrubs, I couldn't shake the similarities to wearing a bright-orange jumpsuit.

The nurse and I left the emergency department and began "the walk." I knew the hospital quite well, well enough to know there were shortcuts and private elevators for people with keys. I finally spotted a clock; it had been over five hours I'd been in that room, alone. It was one a.m. I started to shake and, in a synapse between delusions, began to question why I'd decided to admit myself, yet again.

The paranoia returned. I was aware I knew some people who worked in the hospital, and I wouldn't want to run into any of them, regardless of the hour. She wasn't taking any private routes. I asked her how she got into "the business" and she shared she'd had her own difficulties and wanted to help people. This didn't make me trust her. I sensed an edge to her, a lack of advocacy for my condition. She clearly represented the hospital.

We walked through public corridors dressed similarly but not. My jaw tightened involuntarily. My scrubs carried the markings of a mental patient, and my wrist bore a band reserved for animals, in my opinion. The shame crept up my neck as we walked past the 24-hour in-house McDonald's. I had no appetite, but the smell of onions and grease from the restaurant reminded me I hadn't eaten since yesterday morning.

I felt vulnerable out in the open areas. My feet continued walking next to the nurse while my brain tried to process what was happening inside my head. Twisted and gnarled thoughts fought each other. *What have I done?* collided with *Where's Dr. Malbec?*

We finally reached the last of the public elevators. My consciousness started to fade in and out in spasms. I couldn't tell if we'd gone up or down, but the doors opened. The nurse walked me to a different heavy door, punched in a code, and scanned her lanyard.

"No! I can't do this!" My voice gained volume with each word.

"Everyone is asleep, so please be quiet," the nurse said.

She walked me in, and I heard the door lock behind us. It was then I recognized The Unit. The lights were low. I could see the vinyl furniture. Three phones hung on the wall. The same ancient paperbacks, puzzles, and magazines lay waiting. It was the same room where JD had surrendered a bag of clothes for me and then left. The memories were horrible. *Not this place again; I can't do this.* The cold reality of inpatient treatment crashed through my Malbec fantasy.

The rage I'd jammed to the back of my mind from the recent realizations of abuse to the interminable emergency-department wait erupted suddenly in a loud fury. I would not go quietly into the psych ward. I demanded to be released. The nurse called for help. My knees buckled and panic washed over me. I had made a terrible mistake by coming here thinking they could help. But I'd signed the paperwork, and no one was there to prevent them from keeping me in that locked ward. The last thing I remembered was sensing a pill someone had popped into my mouth and crumpling to the tile floor, surrounded by nurses and security guards.

The nurse had administered a type of tablet designed to dissolve on a patient's tongue in three seconds. This was known as a Zydis dose. The drug, olanzapine, an antipsychotic used to treat schizophrenia and bipolar, was helpful for the staff. Not so much for me, since I'd taken it previously with poor results. Dr. Berger had prescribed it a few years earlier. I couldn't walk straight, and my thought processes became very confused, both then and now. Whether it was a bad reaction to the medication or the hospital environment in general, the next four days were something out of a nightmarish house of horrors.

There are no records of what happened between administering the olanzapine and thirteen hours later. I must have slept and eaten breakfast and lunch, yet I don't recall any of it. I couldn't even manage filling out a menu for myself, so lifting the brown plastic cover at mealtime was Russian roulette.

During this time, I was described as calm, cooperative, insightful, and voluntary. "Voluntary" was simply a status, as opposed to being on a hold. I didn't want to be there. The station I was placed in was slightly less structured and intended for patients who functioned well. It was expected I would attend different therapy groups, make art projects, and follow the rules. That didn't happen.

Thoughts were starting to brew in my brain. I remember being in a group session and having a man show me a picture of a loved one he claimed had been murdered. I laughed. As soon as it bubbled out of me, I thought, *That's not right.* But I had absolutely no control. My emotional governor was scrambled. I felt like my moods were an old movie projector and the film wasn't loaded properly. It would jump, skip, and click, and there was no take-up reel to straighten it.

After the group time, patients were supposed to be docile and quiet and find something to do. This equated to the worst part of inpatient treatment, for me. Unstructured hours on end of mind-numbing boredom provided a perfect breeding ground for my unstable mind to take flight. I made requests of the staff that were denied. Irritated, I went back to my room. The staff decided I needed to be downgraded from Unit 39 to a more restrictive unit. I got triggered by a simple, unsigned note on the message board. It made me scared and I believed someone was watching me, or intentionally trying to frighten me. I was escorted to The Quiet Room. It was one of many trips I'd make.

The "rubber room," a "padded cell," or "seclusion" were also names for it, depending upon whom you asked. For me, it was hell. Each unit had its own version, and I got to know them well.

This one had a light bulb on the ceiling I couldn't control, a mat on the floor, four walls, and a locked door with a small piece of reinforced glass. I can't imagine I accomplished anything more than staring at that single light the entire time. After a few hours, they allowed me to return to my regular room.

My recollections of the times I spent in this Quiet Room are spotty from the trauma and the medications they used on me. But what I do remember, I will never forget. My frustration at my inability to control anything, like my reactions to the perceived slights of the staff or the menu items of my lunch, culminated in a temper tantrum once I was released. I flipped a tray of my meds and dropped an f-bomb at the nurse, which earned me yet another trip to seclusion. I didn't go quietly, so they ordered a bomb of their own.

A B52 is a slang term for an injection of a major tranquilizer, either Haldol or Thorazine, combined with Ativan to ease anxiety and topped off with Benadryl to induce sleep. After they used this drug combination on me, I awoke very confused.

The staff had moved me to a different psych floor. Scrambled and disoriented, I tried to keep it together and follow the rules but instead became frustrated and angry again. I felt like a rat caught in a labyrinth with no way out. I started yelling, scared and mad, and nurses came to restrain me. I was forcibly escorted to The Quiet Room again, this time in the more restrictive Unit 47. They sedated me like an elephant gone rogue. I was left there five hours. When the door finally opened, I was more aware of my environment and the real nightmare began.

The cool, overly conditioned air woke me up. It was ten thirty a.m., but it appeared late at night. The staff had dimmed the lights in the hallway, giving it an eerie, stage-like quality. I didn't recognize the assembled young people in scrubs and uniformed security guards as they closed ranks in a half circle around the door. I struggled to my feet.

I perceived them to be imposters, actors impersonating health-care workers, and told them they were a joke. They whispered to each other, and I gathered it was my bathroom break, but no one said anything directly to me. I was wearing the same scrubs I'd been given two days earlier, but I didn't recognize my own scent. It was rank and sour, completely foreign. But the smell was my clue I was awake.

I darted in the opposite direction of the bathroom but didn't get three paces. The security guards grabbed me by both wrists and wrestled me to the carpeted floor. I felt their fingers press into the flesh around my wrists, and my forearm banged against the hard sole of someone's shoe.

There were strangers' faces hanging over me, grimacing, sweating, and contorting in the effort of pinning me to the ground. The security guard's crotch pressed against my thigh.

"Are you getting off on this?" I screamed. "I'm certainly not." I could not process the dehumanizing terror. I became motionless and went to a place deep inside my mind where my brain wasn't broken.

Do you know who I am? I'm somebody's grandmother. I raised four children. I own two homes, two expensive cars, and throw really fun parties. I came to you for help, and now you're sitting on me and sedating me like an animal. I'm lucid deep inside these eyes. Look at me. I am not a case or a patient. I am a human being.

None of this could be translated to my captors. I was an out-of-control mental patient in a locked ward. They called an emergency code for The Unit. The same code I'd heard years earlier, except now *I* was the problem. The other patients were required to stay in their rooms, supervised by staff from other areas of the hospital, while the psych staff and guards secured me. I learned this from the nurses' notes. I had no realization at the time that my actions had caused the code. I was in survival mode.

I felt my pants tug down, my right hip and butt cheek exposed to the air, then the sting of the needle. Thorazine was the drug of choice, I found out later when I read the report. It was the same drug used on my grandmother in the 1950s. I don't know how they got me back into The Quiet Room because I couldn't walk. They must've carried me.

While I was tranquilized, the psychiatrist assigned to me paid me the first visit since I'd arrived. She chose not to try to wake me because I was sleep-deprived, and she wouldn't have had much luck. She put in her notes I would probably be in the hospital seven to ten more days. And noted I snored loudly.

I awoke hours later, my mouth slack and stuck to the vinyl mat with drool. I had a vague recollection of the night before, but it was so terrifying, I passed it off as a nightmare. Then I saw the bruises. My forearm, wrists, and butt cheek were sore, and I knew it was real. I tried the door. It was locked. I rapped my knuckles on the glass, and a young man in scrubs came up to the door. He had a bemused, insolent look to him, and I asked him politely to release me from The Quiet Room. He refused.

If the definition of *insanity* is "doing the same thing over and over while expecting different results," I certainly qualified. I must've summoned the same man fifteen times, but he never released me. He'd lift the short curtain, mumble something I couldn't understand through the thick glass, and then walk away. I'd been locked in The Quiet Room the better part of three days, but only now was I completely aware of the torturous environment. I was being held hostage by a sadistic gatekeeper. I begged for the password but there was none. I felt trapped, imprisoned, and the troll holding the key was a childish brat. There was no higher authority to call.

The situation reduced me to pace like a stir-crazy animal in a cage. My mind began to use logic to try to free myself. There must be a code, I thought. I had to solve the riddle, assemble the puzzle pieces, find a way. In a cruel inversion, the more progress I made getting my mind to function, the more terrifying the solitary confinement. There was nothing in this room except a cheap mat on the floor. No furniture, no exterior window, only the piece of glass in the door covered by a curtain. Fighting the situation was futile.

The man returned with a deal. If I agreed to sit quietly on the mat and ingest an oral version of the B52, they would open the door. I told him he could suck my dick. This is not typical of the way I speak to people, but I had been pushed too far and I still wasn't well. They injected me with another B52 as my reward for the foul language.

I couldn't figure out what they were giving me, and I decided it was some version of Rohypnol, the date-rape drug. I had sketchy memories and a lot of time blacked out completely. I lay on my back on the thick mat, trying to consciously heal my brain. How was I going to get out of here? It was then I realized my husband and children had no information about my multiple trips to The Quiet Room. They probably thought I was peacefully making God's eyes with yarn and Popsicle sticks in occupational therapy, not locked in seclusion.

I summoned all the wits I could muster and determined the best and fastest way out was to do . . . nothing. I remained still and tried to let the anger dissipate. I sat on the damn mat and waited. Slowly, my thoughts did knit together, and I could sense my self returning. Each minute that passed allowed more healing once I let go of trying to earn my way out.

Finally, twenty-four hours after my latest placement in The Quiet Room, the door opened and I was freed. The staff reminded me it was five thirty a.m., but I had no clue what day. I made no move to run, simply walked slowly behind the nurse. We passed a man she called Doug. He looked remotely familiar. He stared at me with a shocked expression, as if I were an apparition. He was my gatekeeper. I didn't want to acknowledge him, so I held my chin high and looked past him as I returned to my regular room.

Once inside, I found a paper sack of clothes on my desk, along with two notes from my husband. One said, HERE ARE SOME OUTFITS TO MAKE YOU MORE COMFORTABLE. I HOPE YOU'RE HAVING A NICE DAY. I wanted to react with joy and relief at seeing the message, but my emotions were still muted from the druggings. The second note, however, sent chills down my spine. It read, AL'S NOT COMING.

I hadn't told JD about my delusions regarding Dr. Malbec for this episode, yet he knew. It had happened like clockwork every other time my mind went south: (1) talk to God, (2) become distrustful of JD, and (3) think Dr. Malbec is coming and will save the day. My delusions were consistent, at least.

I couldn't grasp at that moment what my hospital stay was like for my husband. He was still shut out of communications regarding my condition. Every time he had called, they not only didn't put the call through, they also wouldn't confirm I was a patient at the hospital. Somehow he'd managed to get notes to me and drop off a bag of clothes without laying eyes on me. With my inklings of sanity returning, I knew he was my real liberator. My first inpatient roommate, Helen, had predicted almost thirty years earlier I should hold on to my dreams of a prince. I just had to realize it was JD.

I went to the desk and rescinded my opt-out directive, which allowed JD full access. It felt wonderful to be in control of my thoughts again. And it gave me hope and a focus to know my husband would advocate for me. I had a long way to go to be well, but I was on the other side of the horrible nightmare.

In a scene right out of *Cinderella Does the Psych Ward*, I found my rose suede slippers at the bottom of the bag JD brought. The leather laces had been removed by the staff as a safety precaution. I discovered the rubber soles of my slippers made quite a loud squeal if I wasn't careful how I stepped. Angry at my treatment and fed up with the hospital environment, I intentionally walked the halls of Unit 47 with my slippers squeaking their wordless defiance.

I ate my meals with the other patients and towed the line as closely as possible for the rest of Sunday. I was eager to get the hell out of there until I realized: Monday was Labor Day. Nothing official happens on holidays at the hospital. That meant no doctor visit, no discharge. I called JD and told him there was a decent chance I'd be discharged on Tuesday, so please make plans with work to be free to come get me. I could tell he was hurt and confused by the silent treatment he'd gotten, but due to his strength and character, he agreed.

My mind returned slowly with the hours that passed. I remembered the items I had surrendered when I first arrived. I inquired at the desk. No one had seen any of it. I channeled all my energy into finding that new book, those journals, notes, and clothes. Six days of unconscionable violations on my mind and body, and now somebody had stolen my stuff. I couldn't show any anger for fear I'd be thrown back into The Quiet Room.

I wasn't simply tasked with recuperation. I had to find my stuff, convince these captors I was okay to be out in the world, follow all the rules and steps to get out, and not get angry in the process.

so ca

Morning broke differently on that Tuesday after Labor Day. With steely resolve, I vowed never to return to that place for an inpatient stay. Everything changed for me because of this visit. The staff were not assistants on my way back to sanity. I had zero association with the interaction of the staff as positive. The smell of the linens' bleach from other visits had reminded me of being cared for. This time it no longer was a source of comfort. I threw off the sheet and blanket and quickly got dressed.

The cart carrying the breakfast trays rumbled onto The Unit, pushed by a nutrition aide. I found my name on the ticket. It rested next to a chrome cover over the lukewarm plate. Knowing I might be leaving still didn't make the eggs palatable. I bussed my tray back to the cart. I sensed they were still watching and charting my every move.

The psychiatrist assigned to me came to The Unit for the first time since Saturday. She looked genuinely stunned at my appearance and demeanor. The last time she'd seen me, I was drooling and unconscious on the floor of The Quiet Room.

I told her my wish to be discharged. She asked if I had a plan. I explained I had my personal psychiatrist to follow me on an outpatient basis as well as a therapist. I was going home to a stable, safe environment, and if I stayed any longer it would jeopardize the progress I'd made. She agreed and signed the discharge, but left me with one caveat: take my time before diving into the sexual abuse revelations that triggered me to come to the hospital. My brain was tender and would need time to heal. I thanked her and ran to find an operable phone to call my husband.

"I got streeted," I whispered into the phone, using the patients' vernacular I'd learned over the years.

"Thank God. Do you know I've been calling multiple times an hour and those bastards wouldn't even acknowledge you were there? I dropped you off and was completely in the dark for days. What's wrong with that place?" he said.

"It was the opt out, JD. It was a mistake to sign it. We can talk about it later. When can you get here?"

"I'll be there at ten o'clock. Please be ready. I don't want you in there a minute longer."

My emotions were dulled by the heavy sedatives; otherwise, I would have burst into tears at his compassion. As it was, I packed the brown grocery bag, including the laceless, squeaky slippers. I left any remnants of hospital toiletries like the lotion or soaps. While the other patients attended Group Time, I showered. My pulse quickened at the thought of leaving, finally.

"May I have a hair dryer to dry my hair?" I inquired of the nurse at the front desk when I'd finished.

"No requests during Group Time," she replied.

"I'm not attending any Group. I'm leaving in thirty minutes. The discharge is signed. Are you telling me you can't make an exception?" I looked at her closely, finding her vaguely familiar in a *Wizard of Oz* sort of way. I knew she had been there when I was jumped outside The Quiet Room. She seemed to want to prove her authority over me regardless of my walking papers.

"No requests during Group Time," she repeated.

I became livid, despite the tranquilizers, and had to remove myself from the situation to remain calm. I went to my room to stare at my paper-sack luggage. The consequences of a temper tantrum at this late stage were too severe. I used the crumpled grocery bag as a focal point, complete with measured breaths, to allow my anger to subside.

I became distracted by noise in the hall. A wave of patients shuffled past my door. I asked where they were headed and they said, "Music Therapy." I decided it couldn't hurt.

When I walked into the room, I was pleasantly surprised. The music therapist, Michael Gardos-Reid, was the same person I'd had as a therapist at my very first hospitalization in 1989. I listened to his choice of music (it may have been Simon and Garfunkel) and tried desperately to let the rest of my anger drain from me as I danced. Some patients sat there and didn't move. Others walked out, frustrated. He came up to me after he dismissed the rest of the participants. I guessed by his expression he could tell I looked different from the others. The life and focus were returning to my eyes.

"What are *you* doing here?" he said.

"I know, right? I had a bad turn of events, but I'm on the mend. I'm being discharged this morning. The woman at the front desk wouldn't let me dry my hair, so I decided to take in music therapy because I love music. And I can't believe you're here. You were here for my first and last trip to the hospital."

I wasn't sure he knew what I meant, yet I was pleased to make the connection.

"Best of luck," he said with a smile.

ꕤ

JD arrived within the hour. We went to the nurse's desk and they produced my purse. I got my ID, credit cards, phone, and cash back in a manila envelope. They also had the pink-tinged white leather laces for my slippers. But my other personal effects were nowhere to be found. JD started to get angry, so I put my hand on his forearm and said, "It's okay."

A nurse brought us out through the locked doors until we reached the public elevators. There was a door next to the McDonald's that exited to the street. I burst past the glass and steel onto the south Minneapolis sidewalk. Although the urban hospital was located close to downtown, the air smelled like sweet freedom to me. Sunlight bathed my face, and a warm fall breeze ruffled the last of the dampness from my hair. I was free.

When we arrived at our townhome in Eden Prairie, I asked JD to come into the bedroom and bring my phone. We took pictures of all the bruises—on my forearm, my wrists, and both hips from the multiple injections. I wanted to document what happened, not for a lawsuit, but to remind us I was never going back there.

For many reasons, it was difficult telling JD what happened to me. I didn't remember all of it, and it was painful for both of us. He felt guilt-ridden for leaving me there, and I felt foolish for signing the opt out in a fit of delusion and petulance. I told him I needed to recuperate in our guest room. I changed into my favorite soft pajamas and fell into the most glorious midafternoon sleep.

Chapter Twenty-Six

Recovery

I wish the trajectory of my healing had been a straight line racing upward from the hospitalization. But, like physical healing, it was hard fought, and for a time, I went backward. I saw Dr. Berger and raged against the system, the hospital, and mental health care in general. He urged me to take care of myself and try to let go of some of the anger. He also handed me my first copy of *bp Magazine*. Stunned to learn there was finally a magazine dedicated to the bipolar community, I devoured almost every word of that issue, skipping only the drug ads.

I convalesced for the first time after a manic hospitalization. In the past, it was always a source of pride to hit the ground running. I had simply ignored the physical as well as mental tolls a hospital stay extracted. Setting myself up in a spare bedroom seemed odd at first, but I told JD the time I'd spent in the hospital felt assaultive, and I wanted to get myself back together without pushing it. While well intended, sleeping alone had its inherent drawbacks.

While I wasn't sick enough to be kept in the hospital, I was not yet completely well. The lingering effects of the manic episode produced high levels of energy combined with a deficit of judgment. Without JD's supervision, I slept odd hours and decided to launch a one-woman social-media campaign decrying the lack of parity in mental and physical health care. Friends and acquaintances were chastised in my blistering Facebook posts, which prompted many phone calls asking if I was okay. I hoped once they spoke to me, my friends would figure out it was one of "those times." The huge majority were supportive and understanding, though I did get a large charge out of one friend. Through a private message, she suggested I get professional help, as if I had never thought of it and it was a cure.

Each day that passed seemed to bring more clarity, and more embarrassment. I googled "how to take down a Facebook post" and successfully did. I also called the Metropolitan Airports Commission and left a recorded message regarding my concerns that the red-and-white Christmas lights recently hung on my house may be distracting to planes. A few days later, a very patient-sounding gentleman returned my call and assured me the lights were not a problem.

Coupled with extreme amounts of mental energy was an incredible impulsiveness. The antipsychotic medications I took weren't completely successful, so I woke one night around three a.m. to the sounds of voices in my room. The whispered words frightened me. Convinced they were intruders, I grabbed my cell phone and called the police. Two officers arrived within minutes and they searched the house. Finding no forced entry or strangers, they left. They, too, were incredibly patient and told me to call if I ever felt unsafe or unsure there was someone uninvited in the house. I was thankful and convinced myself they saved the eye rolling for when they got back to the squad car.

That situation brought on, finally, the realization I had better move back into my own bedroom with JD. I slept through the night and started to regain clarity by the hour. With one last manic burst, I concentrated my energy on sleuthing the whereabouts of my lost belongings at the hospital, in the off chance they hadn't been ripped off. The next day, it took about seven phone calls and many department transfers, but both bags were actually located, in the emergency department. The only catch: I had to personally retrieve them.

I spent all morning getting dressed, made up, and groomed. Full cosmetic armor was necessary to reenter the battleground. I drove to the hospital, parked in the ramp, took a deep breath, and walked into the building as an anonymous guest. The corridors were full of people, and I must've looked as lost and overwhelmed as I felt. A nice-looking man came up to me and asked if he could direct me. I told him I was retrieving some lost items from the ER. He offered to take me there himself. I smiled, thinking this guy had no clue I had been a resident of The Quiet Room a few days earlier. When we arrived, I thanked him for the escort. He had no idea how familiar with the hospital I was or how much I appreciated the chivalrous gesture.

My stuff had never been stolen, simply misplaced. It was all there. As I traced my way out of the hospital, I concentrated on taking deep breaths. It still smelled of disinfectant and alcohol, but I no longer associated the scents with sinister intentions. I realized then I wouldn't allow the place to control me. Those days were over.

Chapter Twenty-Seven

New Rules

JD and I took our long-planned trip to Martha's Vineyard three and a half weeks after my release from the locked ward. It had appeared highly unlikely I'd be in a position to travel so soon after my meltdown, but after I rested and adjusted my expectations, we went in October of 2015. In comparison to my time on The Unit, my brain functioned beautifully. But compared to my baseline, I felt subdued and easily fatigued. To keep me stable, Dr. Berger had prescribed two mood stabilizers, an antipsychotic, an antianxiety, and strong sleep-aid medications. Each of the meds individually had a sedative effect, but cumulatively they left me nearly wiped out.

At a quaint restaurant in the shadow of a lighthouse, JD surprised me with diamond earrings he'd purchased back home and hidden in his luggage. I was overjoyed, truly thrilled. I remember reacting slowly and unenthusiastically to the gift, due to the meds. But the image of the lighthouse got to me.

That was him. Not that we didn't have our moments or communication snafus, considering all that I'd put him through with my jealous raging, distrust, and cyclical fantasies. I had actually been lost at sea, adrift and insecure. He remained steadfast, a shining beacon of love and patience through the years. Without the medications, I would have been consumed with gratitude and crumpled into tears. As it was, I smiled and accepted the jewelry.

I retained vivid memories of the vacation. Taking the bus from Boston, riding the ferry, visiting a small cemetery and seeing the gravestones of many famous writers, attending a play, biking near the beach, and exploring the island by car made indelible imprints.

We were fortunate to stay in a friend's summer home that dated back over two hundred years. I fully understood the global appeal of this small community of respite seekers.

When I got home, I reinvigorated my commitment to *never ever* let anything or anyone get between us. We talked for the first time in years about Dr. Malbec. It bothered me that his specter, even if it was a delusion, could cause me to believe the scenarios I did. The pseudo relationship I conjured up with Dr. Malbec needed to die and be buried. JD and I both acknowledged a vacuum in our marriage had caused the fantasy to fester, but now we had the opportunity to fill the void with a new reality. I gained perspective on my history with Malbec. My memories of him, categorized not with romantic undertones but somewhere between odd and abusive, no longer served any purpose. Once again, and hopefully for all time, I kicked him to the curb.

With that symbolic gesture, it became clear to me what Al Malbec really represented. It took all that heartache to realize I was never infatuated with Al Malbec, the man, at all. He was more than likely flattered, thinking that his dashing handsomeness, enormous brain, or even his bank account was what I coveted. It was none of those traits. That represented gingerbread; a false front.

Did he realize I had scoured my insurance policy in order to discuss my tubal surgery? I'd researched gynecological advances and spotted a new cell-collection device when he used it for a Pap smear. I even mentioned I knew the tool was current. Who does that? I wanted to talk shop and impress him as a professional patient, but deep down I yearned to go to med school and be an obstetrician in my own right.

He proved himself undeserving of my adoration. I no longer saw him as an unwitting participant. In order to justify my obsession with him, I had imbued him with positive traits. The #MeToo conversation helped me to understand how I was one of many. And how the power differential in the relationship had caused much of the pain.

I wanted to see myself as acceptable. If I made him magical, then imagined he loved me, I would be worthwhile. I felt seen by him because that's what I needed: to be chosen, not settled for.

It had never been me running out on my husband. Al was always a figment, a faux affair. My real longing was to find myself and, for the first time in my life, see someone worthy. I can't call what I felt for Dr. Malbec "love." Unintentionally and ironically, when I moved beyond the relationship, it allowed me to realize my true worth.

Reevaluating and hashing over the Malbec saga allowed us to take stock and make new ground rules for other aspects of my care as well. Regarding false pretenses for hospitalization, I gave JD permission to question my reasons if I ever asked to be taken back to the hospital. We explicitly discussed the fact I never wanted to return. I labeled a separate pill box, calling them "the silver bullet meds," which would be my line of defense should psychotic symptoms recur.

As strange as it may sound, after previous hospital stays, we never had a plan for the next one. I always assumed it wouldn't happen again. Taking charge and putting words to fears allowed me to accept the role of gatekeeper of my own mental health. It wasn't up to my family, the hospital staff, or even Dr. Berger to save me from myself. I realized it was up to me.

This was a departure from the way I used to view mental health care. I used to be stuck in the "if only" rut. If only I had a different med, doctor, therapist, or even husband, my life would be so much easier. By not accepting my role as someone who could affect the most change in my own life, I gave away my power.

It was difficult and humbling to realize I hadn't been doing everything I could for myself to stay healthy. It involved a lot more than pills, but that was the first place I made a change. Medication compliance was essential and nonnegotiable for me. I certainly tried to prove that wasn't the case, but my experiment had failed miserably. The absence of a tether allowed my moods free rein to take over my judgment.

Stubbornness and pride had told me I could go it alone, without medications. I figured a weak-willed person would succumb to chemistry lapses, but not my strong brain. In an unfortunate combination of ego, curiosity, and mulish self-pity, I had made the fateful decision to take a break from my meds in 2014. Now, I made the decision they were always going to be a part of my life. Until something better came along, medication was the least I could do to prevent a crippling mania from returning.

ꕥ ꕥ

One of the more alarming conceits of my manic episodes was believing in my own allure. Not only was my long-term marriage disposable during those times, but I had felt that I could marry anyone, due to my irresistible fantasticness. I certainly hadn't grasped the concept that if half of all first marriages fail, a disproportional number succumb when one of the parties has bipolar disorder. The fact I'd been married for over three decades was a testament to my husband and his abilities to see beyond the illness.

Many times, full of hubris and lacking forethought, I'd asked for a divorce over the course of my manic episodes. To illustrate this point, I have to admit it happened again between my discharge from the hospital and our trip to The Vineyard.

There was one reason we never got divorced over the years: my husband. Our marriage was far from perfect, but it withstood the buffeting threats because we never acted on separation impulses while I was sick. Wanting out was predictable, but after the first two or three times, JD viewed it as a symptom of the illness. With this kind of hindsight and the foresight of knowing how wonderful it could be in the future, his deep maturity allowed us to weather the storm.

CHAPTER TWENTY-EIGHT

Becoming a Grown-Up

The night my father died, I turned into a grown-up. Just before midnight on June 11, 2016, my father passed. I hadn't been there. My sister Pat called Teri, Michelle, and me to join the rest of the family at my parents' house. I held my hands to my lips and watched the morticians escort his body, encased in a blue vinyl bag on a gurney, out of his room and through the door for the last time. The rest of the family waited elsewhere in my parents' house. I called upon the experiences I'd had at the hospice and volunteered to be the one to watch his final exit. I cried softly as the lights of the mortuary's unmarked minivan disappeared from view.

The tears fell for what had been and what never was. I felt a rush of nostalgia for the 1969 version, who bought me a shiny, pink bike and carried it down the escalator of JCPenney. And I couldn't deny the physically and emotionally abusive dad whose expectations I never managed to meet. Such a complicated transition death was.

What struck me next were the similarities to birth. In one defining moment he went from one world to the next. Titles in the family changed. When my eldest was delivered, suddenly there were parents, regular and grand. Aunts and uncles stood where siblings once were. The same thing happened when my grandson, Kyle, arrived. Now my father passed into a new realm, and I finally felt elevated to elder.

My father's passing, protracted and expected, with time to say goodbye, left a unique mark on each of my siblings. The family had held vigil for six months at his home-hospice bedside, wondering which day would be his last. I knew I needed to say something to address the abuse as he lay dying. I chose a passive approach.

Knowing I didn't believe the lie we'd agreed to years ago, I tried to release him from admitting his role in the abuse. In February, while he was still lucid, I stood next to his bedside and told him my memories must have been false. I told him I must've been confused. I actually thought my words would give him peace, allow him to let go, to die. He responded, "That's good because I wouldn't be able to defend myself." He surprised me by lasting four more months. We never spoke of it again. I took the statement at face value when he'd said it. The more I turned it over in my mind, the more I started to think it was a cryptic admission of guilt.

For me, his death was a release. It was the beginning of seeing myself through a new lens. No longer daughter to Dad, I finally felt the vessels of my other roles begin to fill: wife, mother, grandmother.

His death meant it was time for me to take responsibility for my own actions and choices. It surprised me it took the actual physical demise of my dad to catapult me into my new strata. As I pored over photos in the following days, the complexities of my relationship with Dad deepened.

Like my siblings, I'd often sought his advice, approval, attention, and love. For me, the counsel-seeking lessened in his later years, yet the need to be a part of his inner circle never did. Dad was a favorites player, which resulted in a tough dynamic for his children. The confliction between what he said—"All are equal"—and what I knew to be true caused me to doubt my ability to trust my intuition and, ultimately, myself.

Over the next few months, I tried to see myself as others saw me. This gave me a better basis in reality, unfettered by my dad's critical voice. I stopped hearing "Stand up straight!" whenever I felt my shoulders droop. My self-image, never fully realized during my father's life, could now expand to include a positive version of me. I saw myself as a supportive friend, a kind and capable person.

From that vantage point, I could stop blaming my dad for my poor self-esteem.

Easing up on blame of all kinds, both of myself, my dad, and others, allowed me to experience compassion. This enabled me to pull out of the self-critical and, frankly, self-absorbed nosedive I'd been in most of my adult life. I'd muddied the concept of trying to gain insight into my bipolar illness by concentrating all my efforts on me. Focusing on *my* pregnant wedding, *my* delayed dreams, *my* strained marriage, and *my* futile fantasy never took into account the other people these events and relationships affected.

Once my dad passed, it became clear to me real change was possible. And it wouldn't kill me to look in the mirror. I feared the weight of holding myself accountable to improve. It felt more satisfying to blame Dad. No doubt, horrible wrongs happened to me as a child, but suspecting abuse and dealing with the reality were two different emotions. I faced them head-on and despite what appeared to be his denials, I found the courage to tell myself the truth.

Although it was easier to blame my dad for my lack of self-esteem and confidence, I began the delicate task of rebalancing my total blame load. Shifting more to myself meant gaining control, while experiencing humility and gratitude. Lifting the responsibility from JD and my parents allowed me to heal the wounds of the past, both as an individual and as a marriage partner.

Understanding I had the keys to unlock my own cage was the mindset change I had to make.

My unwillingness to see that my own life was my responsibility had been a huge roadblock to my recovery, both as a person with bipolar and as an abuse survivor. When I became pregnant for the last time, I had seen myself as a victim of circumstance and my own fertility. My past taught me that life happened to me. Had I known what I was doing, or how to fix it, I would have. That victim mentality had blocked my ability to change. Not the circumstances, but my attitude toward them.

All of that didn't come into focus for me until Dad was gone.

Just like Dorothy in *The Wizard of Oz*, I had the power to change my destiny the whole time. The shadow my father had cast over me during his lifetime only *seemed* impenetrable.

The deluded belief I had been doing everything in my power to get better kept a stranglehold on my progress. Self-pity for having bipolar disorder in my life was not a conscious reaction, but it definitely played a part in keeping me stuck inside the cycle of symptoms.

Counterintuitively, holding myself responsible freed my burden instead of leaving me laden. My perspective needed to switch, and I finally held the reins to my own life. It didn't matter how righteously I believed I had been wronged by my dad. The power to heal remained in my hands and my heart.

Chapter Twenty-Nine

The Happy Times

All aspects of our cabin experience were about healing. The two-and-a-half-hour drive provided JD and me a chance to unwind, talk about our weeks, and reconnect. There was something about the pines and the quiet road that offered the perfect prelude to a weekend Up North. We usually left after dinner on Friday night, stopped at the grocery store in Brainerd, and arrived at our place around ten p.m.

The cabin was more than a retreat. It had a spiritual quality to it. We had furnished it locally with log beds, fresh linens, and a comfy couch with a moose motif. JD and I had lived in four different homes together when we bought the place. Each had their joys and tribulations, but Birch Point was different. It was the first time we started making joint decisions on everything. We retired our "divide and conquer" mantra and chose new colors to suit our tastes, together.

I had sewn curtains for all the rooms that first fall. JD chopped wood for the fireplace. In short order, we transformed a powder-blue-and-white interior with reds, golds, and greens, which gave it a woodsy feel. Our cabin was a year-round sanctuary, and caring for it had healed our marriage. We bought it as empty nesters and were able to create the honeymoon atmosphere we never got a chance to experience when we were young. We took snowy walks in the winter and twilight pontoon rides all summer long.

Interspersed with our alone time, we invited friends and family to visit. Each group had a unique energy, from raucous to subdued, and the variety kept life interesting at the lake. Birch Point was my tether to what was real and important in my life.

An amazing thing about the happiness we created was my attitude toward it. I knew to be grateful and to appreciate everything that kept me out of the hospital. After the nightmare of 2015, it wasn't enough to live each day to the fullest and hope for the best. I needed a strong foundation and an active maintenance plan.

I kept a regular schedule with Sara, my therapist. Some days I'd have a laundry list of problems to explore, and other times I'd check in with routine-maintenance issues to discuss. The most critical element of therapy involved finding someone who knew me and could keep my confidence while she challenged me to be my best self.

Another way I kept up with my self-repair was to invest in my friendships. During the times when I would spiral up into devastating manias, I felt alone and overburdened. It was very easy for me to clam up, scribble some notes in my journal, or take a bath in the middle of the day. I finally realized my friends were a major factor in my successful recovery. The connection I felt in honest, human friendships couldn't be replaced.

My friends gave me feedback when I seemed a little off. For instance, I asked one of them if they thought my reaction to being offended by a former neighbor was commensurate to the perceived slight.

"Not really," Barbara said point-blank. "You seem kind of intense. A little too bright and shiny."

I thought I was doing a marvelous job of hiding the hypomanic feelings that had crept into my life again. I took a risk by asking my friends if they could detect a difference in my mood. That night, I took some meds to counteract the edgy feelings, and I was able to deescalate the mania from taking hold. The crisis never materialized, thanks to my friends.

I realized, finally, the solution to stability in my life was not about keeping busy. I had to take the bull by the horns and learn to look unblinkingly at myself. Blaming circumstances or other people, or feeling like a victim, wasn't going to work in the long run. Giving myself permission to assume responsibility for my decisions and the trajectory of my life gave me back the power I had surrendered years earlier.

Because of my fragile self-esteem, I feared adding the full onus of responsibility would cause me to crack. It turned out that the opposite was true. Grabbing the reins to my own destiny by following a medication schedule, eating healthier, practicing adequate sleep hygiene, and cultivating my relationships gave me agency. Slowly, I turned the lens through which I perceived myself. The image I saw became someone I liked.

☙ ❧

When I'd experienced the recovered memories of sexual abuse, it was the culmination of my life's greatest fear. In the process of reconstructing the circumstances surrounding my first breakdown in 1989, I realized a significant fact that could have contributed. I had learned that members of my extended family on both sides had been molested and raped by a single perpetrator. This had come to light about six months before I fell apart.

The individual had died shortly after I was born. Since I had still been in the safety of the hospital nursery, I figured I was in the clear. He couldn't have gotten to me. Not coincidentally, my first psychotic break happened with ideations of saving the world. I wanted to believe I could redeem my family from the painful legacy I'd just learned involving my loved ones. Before then, I knew nothing about this part of my family history.

The night I thought I was God, I'd pictured my birth had slain the devil. I wanted it to be so. It was a simple allegory, something to lift me up. Unfortunately, there were a lot more demons to slay. I had no ability at the time to conceptualize someone else had abused me. I wanted to be the savior for my family and thought it was a cool idea on God's part to make me Jesus's little sister.

Twenty-six years later, the memories of my own abuse caused yet another fissure in my psyche. I wanted to outrun it, scream it away. I had many other pressing problems to deal with immediately after the revelation, and I'm not going to assert it cleared up in a weekend. Years later, I realized I'd come face to face with my most hideous "what if" and I'd lived past the knowing.

My father never outright admitted to me what he'd done, which I thought would have to happen to allow me to move on. Instead, I took my clues from the brave women of the #MeToo movement and refused to call myself a victim of sexual abuse. The language around this topic is incredibly powerful, and I never could have made it out of the darkness without the ability to see myself as a survivor instead of a victim.

It doesn't change the fact I lived most of my life feeling less than and unworthy. It does allow me to alter the path from here on. I have survived soul-crushing humiliation, being locked in a padded room, and many other difficulties in my life. I survived for a reason. I want to end the stigma.

Facing my fears and coming out on the other side has given me a sense of competence I'd waited my entire life to feel. Sexual abuse, harassment, and power disparity showed itself to me as a teeth-gnashing wolf. In my own way, I stared down the devil and kicked its ass. The New Testament quotes Jesus as having said, "And the truth shall set you free" (John 8:32). I have to agree with my brother on that sentiment.

Chapter Thirty

God

A different aspect of my life that required healing was my relationship with God. I had espoused the idea of the Second Coming, and I was so pleased with the setup: suddenly I had an older brother, Jesus. This thrilled me. He and I would swap stories about our superhuman abilities to cure people, our terrific relationship with Dad, and how much joy we brought to the world. It may sound flip, crass, or blasphemous, but I believed in my heart of hearts it was 100 percent true. I had been called to be the Savior of the Planet.

I thought I was being an obedient daughter to take on the role bestowed on me in the middle of that night. I'd heard, distinctly, the voice I attributed to the being I knew as God, say, "You are my second born. I have been waiting for this moment forever." I came up with Jesus's little sister, and it made perfect sense. It was a new day without precedent, and I was making it up as I went along.

To my dismay, at the time, the healing miracles did not go as well as I'd expected. It had taken until midway through the fourth or fifth day of my initial hospitalization before I relinquished my heavenly tiara, and traded it for the heavy mantel and label of a diagnosed mental patient. After the heyday and euphoria of having a full-on conversation with God, the feeling I was special never fully left. It was like trying to stuff the genie back into Aladdin's lamp.

It was much more pleasurable to be powerful, benevolent, and adored than defective and broken. I wanted to be God. I remember a year and a half after the first breakdown, I listened to

Paul Simon's *The Rhythm of the Saints* cassette in my bedroom while folding laundry. When I heard him sing about Heaven's only daughter, my brain exploded. I had to pull out the insert to verify I'd heard correctly. "It must be true! He's singing about me!" It threw me into a mild hypomanic state. Not full-blown delusional, but I was putting evidence in the "She *is* God" category and ignoring all the reasons why that didn't make sense.

Almost every one of my episodes, both major and minor, had involved the God concept. I got wise to it and learned how to keep my mouth shut during doctor appointments and hospital intake interviews. I developed a "fly on the wall" persona. It was a deal I had with God, to be the boots on the ground. I would find the need and God would do the work. Children and babies would smile at me in stores. They were in on it.

I remember once being in the grocery store while quite high and in a hypomanic state. Supposedly, I needed milk and bread, but secretly I was looking for someone who needed help. It was time to use my superpowers. There was a woman, struggling and having a hard time, who had a toddler with her. I was about to approach the woman and ask if she needed anything, which would have been forward, aggressive, and a boundary incursion. After all, I grew up in the Midwest, and by and large we stay out of other people's business. I looked at the baby, and the little one gave me a look I interpreted as, "Thanks, but no thanks. I've got this." I kept going and went home.

These types of spiritual encounters only happened while I was in a certain state of mania. Stability kept those thoughts tamped way down. If I was too depressed, I wouldn't go out of the house. Too manic, and I was headed to the hospital. There was a sweet spot when it felt like the universe would come together for a short time and allow me to take a peek at a place or time most people never get to experience. It felt like a portal to heaven.

I was loved. God existed and I was a close, personal friend. Everything was possible. But early in my treatment, after a revolving door of therapists, I grew weary. When I decided to explore the religious aspect with my psychologist Susanne, she'd wanted a lot of details. I was to fill out a journal with different-colored pens, in order to differentiate God's voice from my own. Of course, the voice stopped. I described as many of my "I see God *everywhere*" stories as I felt comfortable and soon felt unburdened. I wanted to, needed to, trust someone with this, and since I was paying her, she seemed a reasonable resource.

Recalling to Susanne my divine history, I described a party at a friend's house over a year earlier, where my friend was lamenting how she was having some fertility issues and was horribly frustrated. One of the women jokingly said, "You should talk to the goddess herself." Everybody laughed and pointed to me. It was all good natured because these friends knew nothing about my healing preoccupation and only that I'd had four babies in six years. In front of at least five people, I put my own blessing on my friend's forehead. Within the year she delivered twins.

When I finished the story, Susanne scoffed. Then I told her it happened again. Another friend conceived after she'd sought a blessing from me, mostly in jest, but she was open to it. The therapist's only response was, "Well, that little trick wouldn't make you too popular in an elevator, would it?" Despite her tone, I could tell she was intrigued.

I became conflicted. I wanted to help people and I wanted to be special, but I also wanted desperately to be normal. Having God as a friend came with huge responsibilities. I would have loved to be a buffet-style mental patient, taking the best elements from the illness and leaving the frightening, debilitating features that made my life hell.

When I went back for my next therapy appointment, after having revealed my God stories, Susanne and another female doctor mysteriously showed up in the waiting area. I saw Susanne cock her head toward my chair. It was obvious she'd shared my story and was pointing me out to the other woman. I kept quiet until we were back in the session room. Burning with rage, I confronted her.

"What was with the head nod in the lobby?"

"What do you mean? I'm not sure what you're referring to."

"Yes, you do. You told that woman about me and then pointed me out of the crowd."

She knew she'd been discovered. We both did. She'd broken the confidentiality of the therapy. As she fumbled through her lame explanation, my mind raced. *Why has she done this? Does she believe me? Or worse, am I just an oddity, someone to joke about in the staff room?* I felt betrayed by Susanne and vowed to never speak of the God thing to another therapist or psychiatrist again. I got up and quit her on the spot.

I bought books on near-death experiences, angelic interventions, and world religions. I became absolutely desperate to find someone like me in order to validate my experience. Just when I thought I would hit a nerve of recognition by finding my story in a book, the author would emphatically extricate their subject from mental illness. There was no resource that would allow the taint of a mental health diagnosis to sully their research. No one, it seemed, wanted to be associated with "those crazy people."

so cs

In 1992, I went to visit my parish priest, Fr. Tim Power. His advice was to read a dirty book and get my head out of religion. He sympathized with my story and even told me that the dream I'd had two weeks before I fell apart (in which God foretold my breakdown) was absolutely real. God had reached out to me in peace and love. The rest of it was basically my brain run amok. If anyone knew God's intention, it would be Father Tim. I left disappointed.

A few years later, I wanted to give it one more try. I made another appointment with Father Tim. He was extremely busy, a popular and gifted man. As the day of the meeting drew near, I prepared to share everything I could think of, but I was afraid he would turn me away too. The night before we were supposed to meet, he called to tell me he had to reschedule because of a double funeral he had to prepare for. An elderly woman had died, and as the family was arriving from various parts of the country to pay their respects, her husband died too. He asked me to ponder how exceptional that timing was, a couple dying almost on cue, and if I could please come see him the following Thursday. Never a believer in mere coincidence of any sort, I couldn't refuse.

At his office, I refreshed him on my story. When I mentioned I had bipolar disorder, he winced and said, "What a cross," which is Catholic for, "I'm so sorry. That's a terrible burden." I immediately felt relief. No psychobabble, no DSM to consult for a diagnosis, no judgment as to my worthiness, and certainly no lecherous overtones. This man was a safe harbor. But I only had one shot left to tell him my version of events.

He listened to my story and, amazingly, found a biblical solution: John the Baptist. He recalled how so many people had approached St. John with the notion he might be God. He quoted the passage where John refutes this idea and says, "I am not the Messiah." And he also said simply, "I am not" (John 1:20–21). Father Tim told me to repeat that to myself the next time I started thinking I might be Jesus's sister. He shook my hand and showed me out.

As I was walking through the parish office area, filled with administrators, he burst through his office door, laughing. He had an Irish twinkle in his eye when he looked at me and boomed out: "I am not!" I half waved and slunk out, suddenly embarrassed from the blast of attention.

It took me many years to figure out what all of that meant. One of his explanations for why I wasn't God was: He doesn't operate that way. God would never single out a person with such a responsibility without giving them a support staff or notifying other people that God was back on Earth. But when he took a beat to think about it, he'd told me, he thought it was very creative. He hadn't laughed at me, like I originally thought, he laughed *with* me.

He was a very liberal, inclusive, and generous man. Often, he was at odds with the patriarchy in the Church. He passed away in September of 2016, a few months after my dad, and I wept at his funeral. There were times, years later, when I recalled his dancing eyes as he belly laughed when I left his office. If God were to come back, as a mentally ill person, a woman, and knock on Tim's door for help, the priest might have found that grand indeed.

No matter how hard I'd wished or how much evidence I'd piled up to the contrary, I was not God. I shook my fist at God many times for pulling the rug out from under me and allowing my brain to imagine such a thought. Eventually, about twenty years after diagnosis and untold number of God visits, I stopped being angry and frustrated.

Sure, it was odd and maybe unfair to come so close to nirvana only to run out of chain and get snapped back to reality. But at least I had experienced it. And in the space between, life was reasonable. I sought out many opinions to have another human validate my spiritual experiences. It felt like learning to balance on a tight rope. I gained confidence in my humanness and began to let go of the need to be the Almighty. I started to appreciate the gray areas. It wasn't all madness, illness, or purely mystical. It was a tangled-up ball of all of the above.

I had to stop concentrating on how many times I fell and look instead at the help I got to get back on my feet. My wonderful husband had stood by me, my fantastic children welcomed me back into their lives without rancor after each episode, and my friends that knew never missed a beat. I needed a lot of help from my village. And my version of God? It's a lot more personal than some people's, but I own it. I no longer offer it up to be judged, condemned, or blessed.

Another meaningful aspect in how I view God is through the power of friendship. Growing up with my siblings around me and changing schools often, I had a difficult time making friends. Throughout my life, and especially after I was diagnosed, I had to force myself to open up and be vulnerable. The rewards have been overwhelming.

I not only have friends who sustain and support me but also am fortunate enough to have layers of women around me. Whether it be walking around a city lake, playing mah-jongg, discussing politics and books, or heading out for a girls' weekend, I have a reliable network in place. It's definitely one of the key factors in determining the quality of my life and the secret to my successful recovery. I am extremely grateful to God to have these women in my life today.

I was so far gone, lost, and hopeless in the course of my illness that I had given up on God at times. But the entity I know has been there through all my battles and has never let go of me. In my darkest times, when I thought God needed a therapist, I would listen to the voice for hours. I never described those instances to my own care team because I was ashamed. I also assumed they'd try to explain it away in a fashion that deemed me psychotic and less than.

I believe God has given me a lot of challenges but also more gifts to deal with them. When my time is up—and I'm in no hurry—I expect to have another conversation with God. This one will involve answers to my questions, a lot of wine and laughter, and a beautiful warm embrace.

Chapter Thirty-One

The Concept of Five

Oh, how I longed to be a five. Not to be confused with the ubiquitous five-star review, this five is smack in the middle. Warm, not frozen or boiling, would suit my Goldilocks standard. From my earliest memories, I had no concept for simmer; I had two speeds: off and high.

I mistook my bipolar style for excitement. It was actually chaos. I resented people who weren't wrapping gifts at two a.m. on Christmas Eve. They weren't as busy or as generous as I. Where is the thrill without the big flourish of coming in at the wire?

To me, bipolar only affected my family when I had to leave and be cared for in the hospital. It was impossible for me to understand the impact I had on them while I was home. I blocked out the chronic tardiness, obsession with details, irritability, and when I was really depressed, three baths a day.

I referred to an episode the other day as "one of the bad ones." Lauren corrected me. "Mom, they were all bad." JD reminded me not to recall the manias as hurricanes. Hurricanes you see coming; you have time to take precautions. He insisted they were much more like tornados. "One minute it's a beautiful day, then the sky darkens and *bam!* There goes your house."

JD introduced me to the idea life could be lived happily at five. He has been the epitome of consistency. Routine has always been his driving force, and he has used it successfully. When we first started living together, I challenged his methods. "Where's your sense of urgency?" I would taunt, frustrated at his lack of last-minute panic. It was completely outside of my experience someone could be that prepared.

He was not the type to ask, "How's that working for ya?" when I found myself perpetually behind the eight ball. He chose not to follow my lead emotionally and has consistently refused to buy into my style of rushing around in a frenzy every time I need something done. He gets up at the same time every day. He thrives in the five zone.

I wish there was a magic threshold I'd crossed over so I could pinpoint when I decided five was the goal. The closest thing I can come up with is the time Dr. Berger gave me a mood scale to chart my behavior. Zero was the baseline, with ten degrees in either direction. I knew plus ten all too well. I didn't spend a lot of time in the negatives, but I had an immediate distaste for labeling myself less than zero. I stared at the chart and focused on the five.

When I would come in for a med check and triumphantly report I had been a five, Dr. Berger would give me a double take. I would have to remind him I use the scale differently. Zero through three would indicate a low or depressive mood. Four, five, and six were in the neutral range. Seven was hypomanic, and nine or ten meant way too high. Self-monitoring my moods took a lot of diligence and required me to gain insight into my personal version of bipolar disorder. I dwell in six to ten, in general, more often in the spring and fall.

What amazed me was my ability to predict the upswing of mania and cut it off at the pass. I had the option of using meds to clear up my thinking or drastically curtailing the stimulation my brain got and heading to bed. As I got better at charting my moods, I could see these manias didn't actually come out of nowhere. When sixes became nines on the mood scale, it was time to make adjustments, or risk going to a place mentally where the moods would affect my behavior and thinking.

Moderation is a word bandied about our house a lot. JD started saying it to the kids as a lighthearted admonition against celebrating too hard on their twenty-first birthdays. Ironically, he never said it to me under any context, but I realized it could be used for every aspect of my life in my quest for five.

Once I decided moderation worked as a mantra, I slowly applied it to eating and sleeping. Don't get too hungry. Don't eat until you're uncomfortably full. Don't stay up until four a.m. (I had to start somewhere.) You most probably don't need fifteen hours of sleep. I'm still in the process of tweaking my diet and slumber schedule, but I have a much better idea of what keeps me in the groove of stability.

Shopping is still a problem. I think someone should come up with a governor or some controlling device for online shopping. When I was attempting to learn how to quilt (unsuccessfully), my sewing teacher said, "Nothing worthwhile happens in the sewing world after midnight." I believe that holds true of buying as well.

JD laughed at the Vraylar® drug commercial depicting a woman in the throes of mania buying multiple expensive cameras. I found it painful. Impulsive shopping is addictive, easy, and horribly damaging to a bank account and relationships. I personally think chronic spending is more prevalent than alcohol addiction, but people turn a blind eye and call it "a robust economy."

When stores never close and items are delivered to your door seven days a week, it can be difficult to self-manage buying and spending. The over-the-top nature of the illness doesn't do well in that environment.

Buying goods I wanted seemed to salve the wounds of a deprived childhood *and* feed the dopamine rush I got from hitting the "submit order" button. Early on in my career as an overspender, I would peruse catalogs of clothes. I had to write down the item number, size, and price, then call a live operator who took the order. Ten days later a box would arrive with my outfits and an updated catalog. I remember ordering again before I even got the other stuff unpacked.

I don't recall consciously thinking, "I deserve this," but I do know it felt wrong. I would destroy the packing materials and break down the boxes before JD got home from work. It didn't occur to me it could be part of my bipolar illness, either. There had to be individuals with bigger-ticket items that caused more disruption, I rationalized.

In a hypomanic state, I felt like one of those mice in the psych experiments that hit the button for more cocaine instead of food. The smell of new clothing and the sounds of unwrapping a fresh box fueled the shopping addiction. When my mind spun into mania, I had no need for earthly possessions. I went up into the realm of communicating with God. Depressive times slowed everything down. "Why would I buy anything for someone so undeserving and fat?" said my confused conscience.

The shopping component was insidious and usually well out of control by the time I recognized it. I became so convinced I deserved all the largesse the universe intended for me that I had a horrible time restricting my desire for clothes, shoes, jewelry, and even office supplies.

I didn't want to deny the kid inside who never had the right maxi dress, tight white go-go boots, or saddle shoes. It took a physical collapse of the bracket in my walk-in closet to fully illuminate my issue. A loud cracking sound came from my closet, followed by a deafening thud. The bolts ripped out of the drywall, and my clothes were scattered in a heap. It was a concrete example of overindulgence, overspending, and a bloated amount of stuff. In a monumental turn of perspective, I reframed what it meant to care for myself.

Determining an actual need took a lot more discernment. I practiced the art of resisting the impulse, both in-store and at home on the computer. Using the image of the child that went without in her formative years finally got retired. Casting my eyes over the sheer number of items I'd purchased brought feelings of guilt and shame, completely offsetting the thrill of the buy. Although I still occasionally indulge myself or my family, a necessary awareness has settled in to stanch the flow of cash out the door. Actually keeping track of the times I skipped buying something felt like I was saving money.

Very recently, after close to twenty years of financial free rein, I decided I had maxed out on spending. As I drove home from an errand near a retail area, I made a mental list of what I needed. I couldn't come up with anything. That was probably the first time ever. It felt amazingly satisfying to just say no.

Once I figured it out, that my happy place is in the vicinity of five, life got a lot easier. It's not deprivation to be less than overstuffed. It's not going without to eschew my favorite sweater in every color. This may not seem very "aha" if you've never had difficulty with overdoing it, but to me it was a big deal. Moderation worked for me once I recalibrated my satisfaction meter.

My relationship with money, food, time, and sleep always felt bipolar. "All or nothing" wasn't just my battle cry, it was how I approached almost everything. Moderating one area successfully allowed me to apply the same attitude toward the next, and soon I had achieved a lifelong goal: a manageable life. Five wasn't something to deride as boring or predictable. I took the pejorative attitude off "the middle" and stopped thinking I was destined to ride the roller coaster of "extreme" forever.

I believe in medication. The healing that comes from meds can be nothing short of miraculous. But in and of themselves, they can't be expected to cure me. I take daily mood stabilizers as a safety net and to provide my brain with maintenance. I've experimented with my doses over the years, and it always ended poorly. There was absolutely nothing in my system to prevent another manic episode from ravaging my life in 2015. I held out longer than expected, but the stress was cumulative, and I paid the price in every way possible.

Discovering the path to stability ended up fraught with stubbornness, hubris, confusion, and raw pain. I understood it was tremendously easier to tweak my moods from a place of three or seven on my mood scale than when I was flying high or couldn't get out of bed. I'm also not interested in tempting fate any longer. So, I take the meds. I've found relief from antipsychotics when the mania gets unmanageable. Checking out for a day to reset and sleep is highly preferable to embarrassing myself or my family.

It's not necessary for me to clutch the dragon's tail and hang on for dear life to prove I can take it. That's no longer how I measure personal success. I've been manic and high enough times to discern "happy" from "euphoric," and when to call the doctor.

Dr. Berger will listen to my symptoms and advise me on dosages and timing. It's a skill and an art. The reset usually takes a day, two at the most. This is way shorter than the duration of a common cold and amazingly preferable to a hospital stay. I rely on his expertise, while he trusts and respects my insight. We're a team, and the respect works both ways. I don't stay up until three forty-five a.m. three nights in a row, and then call him in a panic. I firmly believe in being a responsible mental-wellness patient.

I'm also scared straight. If I require hospitalization, I would no longer be in Dr. Berger's jurisdiction. I'd have to be followed by whomever the doctor on call happens to be, which could be a crap shoot. There was no such thing as prevention in the early days of my diagnosis. I felt like I was doing everything in my power, by taking the meds alone, to stave off another episode. Now I realize I have a lot more in my arsenal than I thought.

Journaling is also helpful but does not replace human interaction. A trained therapist will provide essential feedback and not simply be a dumping ground for ranting. I appreciate the opportunity Sara gives me to choose my topics to explore. A combination of support and challenging my beliefs, especially about myself, have been keys to successful therapy.

I had to work my way through multiple iterations of meds, management, and therapists to get to a combination that worked for me. Helpful doctors and therapists are difficult to find, and sometimes, to keep. But if it wasn't working, I owed it to myself to keep trying. I don't believe doctors or psychologists, alone, can save anybody. It has to be a partnership.

I believe in being an expert on one's own version of bipolar disorder. Today, there's a vast array of knowledge available through various sources. But what I know about myself and how I function when stressed is unique to me. The more personal insight I bring to the equation, the higher the probability I can be successful in treating my illness. If both of my care team members quit tomorrow, I'd be sad. But I wouldn't be lost. Now I can tell any new therapists or doctors, "This is not my first rodeo."

Another element insight helps with is confidence. I will never again fall for an ego-driven doctor, in any field, who doesn't have my best interest at heart. I spent too many years putting up with subpar treatment at the hands of professionals because I didn't know any better. Or worse, I didn't think I deserved to be treated like a peer. I do.

As of this writing, it's been five and a half years since my last hospitalization. This time, I've taken concrete steps toward making my life more stable. There are no guarantees, but I've never felt better. I could weep when I think of all the pain and suffering I put my loved ones, especially JD and my children, through as I navigated the bipolar world. But that's not helpful. Hopefully, I have a lot of my life left to live. I want to model for them and others that a diagnosis of bipolar disorder doesn't give a person a free pass to mess up their life. There is a way out if you seek it.

Chapter Thirty-Two

Re-Newlyweds

Forty years ago, I was a reluctant bride. I wanted more time to prepare, different circumstances. I was too young, too scared, and incredibly . . . lucky.

At the time we were married, we didn't know each other very well. I had yet to realize the depth of JD's commitment or how his loyalty would buoy me. He had no concept for how strong I was or the demons I'd eventually conquer. Time has now told me the answer to the *Let's Make a Deal* question of whether I'd chosen wisely to marry my boyfriend of one year. The answer is a resounding yes!

When we took our vows, JD had no idea how much the sickness-versus-health ratio would be skewed. Neither did I, for that matter. Over the course of my illness, he had a few friends advise him to "cut bait." Fortunately for both of us, he chose to stay. To this day, I can't hear George Michael and Aretha Franklin sing "I Knew You Were Waiting (for Me)" without getting weepy.

JD always worked hard to provide for his family, and there were instances in the early years when it consumed him. We were busy going in separate directions. We lost sight of each other's needs. I checked out emotionally and went searching for the attentions of someone else. I thank God that fantasy wasn't physical, or it might have been fatal to our marriage.

It would be natural to think we'd be better off without the hardships of mental illness and emotional infidelity in our marriage. I would have loved to live out that scenario, but it wasn't an option. Like steel galvanized by fire, our relationship withstood everything fate threw our way. We didn't simply survive the tests, either; we both came out changed.

We had to rebuild our foundation multiple times. There were instances when I feared our union wouldn't withstand the threats, but an intangible element provided the binding agent that kept us together. It was faith. Not a blind piousness locking us into a pledge we'd made in our twenties. It was hope. The leap-of-faith kind of belief. I can't bottle it or sell it, yet we both have it in spades.

He's not perfect, and I'm certainly not a total albatross. We still fight over stupid stuff, except now there's a safety net that prevents a free fall. It's a willingness to see the other side. We developed the ability to take a step back and ponder where the hostility is coming from instead of lashing out. When I get really mad, I remind myself, "This is my person. He deserves my respect, and I need to treat him with care." If I take a breath, I'll discover I'm actually feeling hurt, tired, or hungry, and I'm taking it out on my husband because he's nearby.

Another reason the marriage endured was our practice to never legitimize divorce talk while I was actively manic. JD had the emotional intelligence and foresight to deal with those episodes for what they were: a symptom of my illness. I was sick, even though I looked okay and at times could pass for rational. What goes up definitely comes down, and I could cry myself to sleep thinking of how close I came to throwing away my past and future.

On our vacation to Martha's Vineyard, we recalled our early married days with kindness, to ourselves and each other. We weren't ready to get married in 1981, and we definitely lacked the tools to express what was in our hearts. In the past, guilt and fear prevented any discussion of negative feelings. The prevailing wisdom was "if we don't talk about it, it's not real." We both finally allowed each other to say we had felt trapped by the situation, but it didn't lead to the conclusion we shouldn't have gotten married or that we should get divorced.

It feels like we snatched our marriage from certain defeat, and now we think of ourselves as "re-newlyweds." It doesn't diminish anything by saying we work at it. I had to abandon my juvenile fantasies about how love and marriage operate; it *is* work. And that's not a bad thing.

JD was my first love. The disaster that was Dr. Malbec was an infatuation but served a purpose. Unintentionally, that pseudo relationship led me to understand what I had been seeking the whole time: I needed to come back to me. I snapped, cracked up, and mended so many times, but in the end I prevailed. With the support and enduring love of my husband, I finally love myself. I have become another love, The Second.

I never achieved the compensated career goals I thought would make me happy. Four decades after starting out my marriage as a skills-challenged housewife, I am now an official kick-ass homemaker. My holiday meals can be counted on, and I possess an encyclopedic knowledge of home care. I espouse the identity I created, with a strong sense of pride in what I've achieved.

My children are all grown adults now. The circumstances of their upbringing couldn't have been easy. I purposefully didn't bring their viewpoints into this story to protect their privacy. I didn't want to speak for them, either. They are four individuals with separate perspectives on how my illness affected their lives. What binds them is their collective empathy for others and their resilience. They also know themselves. We raised them to follow their own dreams, and that's what they're doing. They make me proud every day.

Epilogue

In earlier versions of this story, Dr. Malbec played a more prominent role. My beta readers informed me they "got him" early on and more evidence wasn't necessary. I saw him many times, intermittently, over the course of seventeen years. I have a lot of notes to document the encounters, but now that's the past.

To describe in any more detail would reveal Dr. Malbec as a specific individual. It's not important who he is because he represents something much larger than himself. I have to reconcile my role in all of this and at the same time realize the social conditioning women endure. How they see themselves also plays a part. On the other hand, there are women who walk out on the Dr. Malbecs of this world after one visit. I now see that as an appropriate response and one I never had in my arsenal.

Dr. Malbec still practices medicine, as far as I know. Like a lot of people, he has his detractors and rabid fans. Now that I've told my story, I am at peace.

Coming to terms with my illness and choosing to be public about it has equalized the pressure inside of me. It was stressful trying to fit into society while feeling outside of average. There may be nobody actually inhabiting the normal stripe, yet I find solace in knowing I am living my truth. My inner life is aligned with what I present on the outside.

Something like what happened to me may not have touched your family, but if it has, I want you to know you're not alone. The stigma of mental illness is real, and I believe if more people tell their stories, it lessens the fear and judgment. Thank you for choosing to read mine.

Two happenings occurred that illustrate how far JD and I have come, and I'd like to end with them. The second Saturday in

January of 2020, I attended an event that blew my mind. I saw Oprah Winfrey, in person, at an arena stop in Saint Paul on her 2020 Vision tour. I went alone, reveling in the moment, having waited my entire adult life to experience my personal idol and have the spiritual experience wash over me.

As I left the event, I called my husband. I told him the day was magical, everything I'd hoped. He understood what Oprah meant to me, how integral to my recovery I'd felt she'd been, and he and I shared a moment as my car rolled down the freeway toward home.

When I walked in the house, the kitchen island sparkled. The hardwood floors were swept and mopped. Clean laundry was folded neatly on our expertly made bed, complete with accent pillows in their proper place. JD wrapped me in his arms.

"Welcome home. I'm so glad you got a chance to finally see Oprah," he said.

I hugged him tightly.

Grabbing him by the forearms, I looked directly into his eyes.

"You did all of this for me. I know it's *you* who sees *me*. You are my gift. And for all you do, and for who you are, I am forever grateful."

ꟿ ☙

In November of 2020, the world had been upended by COVID-19. JD arranged for me to stay in a luxury hotel in downtown Minneapolis to finish editing this book. I curled up in the expansive space, surrounded by journals, binders, notes, and timelines. The scent of the white sheets and towels reminded me of the hospital in a tangential way. Except those days were over. I'd transcended those experiences. Nothing remained but the stories and the resilience of surviving. I'd lived to tell.

RESOURCES

Helpful Tips for Managing Bipolar Disorder

In this section of the book, I will share some of the techniques I've learned over the years to manage and mitigate the effects of bipolar disorder. I have been diagnosed with Bipolar I, the most severe version of the disorder. All I needed to qualify was one or more manic episodes, lasting at least a week or requiring hospitalization. Check that box. I'm also in the subset of rapid cyclers. These are individuals experiencing four or more mood swings in a twelve-month period. To top it off, I have psychotic features, or breaks with reality associated with my manias. Not all people who have bipolar disorder are in that camp.

Bipolar II is another version of the disorder. People with this diagnosis are more likely to have depressive episodes and at least one hypomanic episode. Hypomania is by definition less severe than a full-blown manic episode, but the behavior will stand out as more energetic and intense than normal for that individual.

While not all these symptoms may apply to you, I believe recognizing you have an issue with mental illness is the first step. If you think anything discussed in this book pertains to you, please advocate for yourself and seek professional help. A competent and thorough evaluation is a place to start.

Community Resources

The following websites are places to find information on mental health and bipolar disorder:

1) National Alliance on Mental Illness (NAMI)
   Nami.org
   National organization for people affected by mental illness and their loved ones.
   State and local offices available in some areas.
2) The Depression and Bipolar Support Alliance (DBSA)
   DBSAlliance.org
   National group supporting people affected by depression and bipolar affective disorder.
   State, local, and online support available.
3) *bp Magazine*: Hope & Harmony for People with Bipolar
   BPHope.com
   Print and digital magazine dedicated to serving the bipolar community; also helpful for family members and loved ones.

I would also recommend seeking resources from the #MeToo movement if you need support for sexual harassment or abuse: https://metoomvmt.org/explore-healing/resource-library/

Best Practices

Sleep Hygiene

Above all else, my best defense against the onset of manic symptoms is to get enough rest. Sleep is something to guard religiously. It took me a long time to realize that staying up late, sleep disturbances, or burning the candle at both ends will result in triggering my brain into overdrive. At that point, no mood stabilizers will prevent an episode. Preparing myself for sleep with a warm bath and limiting screen time before bed is also helpful.

A regular sleep routine is best. It's also helpful to chart sleep to detect mood disturbances. Becoming aware of patterns is essential in recognizing problems before they get out of hand. There are apps available to help with this.

Medication Compliance

Taking my prescribed medications has been essential in maintaining stability. Where it may not affect my moods immediately, the nature of the medication regimen is more like a firewall. Without it, my brain's ability to right itself when stressed is extremely compromised. I don't contend it's easy, due to side effects like lethargy and weight gain, but it is necessary. For the record, I have lost weight while taking antipsychotics and mood stabilizers. It requires discipline and perseverance, but it is completely possible.

Self-Care

The practice of self-care is highly individual. That's the cool part of it. Prioritizing efforts to both calm yourself and spend time getting to know what works in your particular situation will bring wonderful rewards in maintaining mental health. My brother Brian worked with me for the past two years on a program dedicated to self-care. I've done meditation, music therapy, art therapy, special attention to my feet, aromatherapy, ambient-light therapy, journaling, and my favorite pastime: taking a scented bath.

I have a room in my house I call my sanctuary. I set the lighting, use an essential-oil diffuser, and basically fill the space with a comforting energy to meditate. I choose music and listen on headphones in a darkened atmosphere conducive to relaxing. I have already made remarkable progress destressing and making connections with myself in areas I needed to be healed. I have a type of tether now that had been missing in caring for myself.

Understanding Impulse Control

Getting a handle on extreme behavior in all forms has made my life more manageable and livable. I have discussed my relationship with spending at length, so I'll add that limiting the opportunities to make impulsive choices has been helpful. Structure and routine have become preferable to jamming my days with multiple activities and then lying around trying to recover. I have learned to budget my energy for big projects. Chipping away at my goal helped me to finish this book. I may always have trouble trying to do too much in too little time; now it's, hopefully, the exception rather than the rule.

Satiety

Understanding and learning moderation introduced an entirely new sensation: the concept of satiety. I had a similar relationship to food as I did with spending. It also took an exceptionally long time to realize the two were connected. I learned about satiety from a woman whose course I took in order to clean up my diet, get active, and, hopefully, lose weight. She asked me to keep a food journal, recording mindfully how I felt after eating. The goal was to identify and repeat the feeling of *hara hachi bu*, a Japanese proverb, roughly translated as "to eat until your belly is 80 percent full" and popularized by Dan Buettner in his 2008 book, *The Blue Zones.* My bipolar stomach had no concept of this. I was either starving myself, which happened during certain phases of hypomania, or foraging for everything in sight. I ate until I was uncomfortably full, waited a few minutes, and then craved something sweet.

Of course, this led to massive weight gain. By the time I sought out the woman's help, I was almost double my lowest adult weight. We worked for weeks on eating organic foods, limiting portions, eliminating sugar, and adding exercise. The program was wonderful, but I failed miserably. The timing wasn't right.

The concept of satiety stuck with me as a goal, however. It gnawed at me, but it felt out of my realm of possible. I had a difficult time loving and accepting my heavy self while simultaneously yearning to improve my health. Getting down on myself for being fat didn't make the weight fall off any faster. For me, I reached a precipice. The size I wore was the last one offered without the dreaded *W*. Once I expanded into that category, my style choices would be limited and, frankly, not resemble the garment as pictured.

Only recently, after my entire life had been spent in extremes, have I been able to espouse the middle ground. I am learning the feeling of putting the food aside before my stomach is fully satisfied. It may sound stupidly obvious, but that is a game changer to a charter member of the clean-plate club.

Healthy Eating and Activity

I can't always say I'm a perfect example of this, but it is a goal. Limiting sugar is a place to start in maintaining mood control. Fresh foods, especially vegetables, are a preferable antidote to fast food and processed meals. Not only is it smart to fuel your body with a clean diet, but I can attest to having an easier time with my mental health.

Last, but of utmost importance, is getting regular physical activity. Walking has been a win-win for weight control and shaving the highs and lows. I read somewhere that Charles Dickens, who may also have had bipolar disorder, used to take walks on his estate grounds. Whether or not that's true, I'm still in good company. Used as a tool, regular exercise is incredibly effective in releasing endorphins and the production of serotonin. That way, my body gets accustomed to a moderate rush instead of a geyser of dopamine. The key is, again, moderation and consistency.

Acknowledgments

First, I'd like to thank JD. I have no idea where I'd be without you. Your enduring love and support are the stuff of legend.

Lucas, Lauren, Sophie, and Will have been amazingly supportive of their mother and this project yet have never read a word. I appreciate your trust.

My grandson, Kyle, who chose his own pseudonym, has been a wonderful cheerleader and source of joy.

A big shout-out to Phil and Helen for joining our merry band and allowing me to view our collective from fresh eyes.

My mother, Jeannette, for modeling strength, grace, and determination.

My boisterous Burns family siblings: Teri, Pat, Maureen, Michelle, Michael, and Brian.

My ever-patient book club, who waited over twenty years to read this selection.

My amazing friends: The Dynasty/Moonlighting Club, The Mah-Jongg Mavens, Christmas Card A-Listers, Sorority Sisters, Loft writing group, and the Theme and Voice writing group.

My beta readers.

My incredible trialogue.

My "aunties" Roann Mezzenga and Loraine Mezzenga and my brother-in-law John Durda for their enthusiastic support of my writing. They all went to heaven before I could finish the book. Their faith in me buoyed the project through to completion.

A big thank-you to my Loft Literary Center teachers, especially Kate St. Vincent Vogl and Mary Carroll Moore, who encouraged me to persevere through some incredibly rough drafts.

Marion Roach Smith, who taught me about memoir, structure, and discipline.

I also want to thank Tye Biasco for consultation services.

I'm grateful for my all-female team of collaborators who helped me birth this book:

Lynn Post, copy editor
Karen Parkin, proofreader
Julie Klein, book interior designer
Danna Mathias, cover designer
Mi Ae Lipe, publishing consultant

To Oprah Winfrey, Brené Brown, Glennon Doyle, and Mel Robbins: Your work sustained me when I faltered. You don't know me, yet I feel I know you.

And a special thank-you to the following people I know well. You reached out to me at critical times and kept me going. Your kindness touched me deeply and profoundly, and for you I am truly grateful:

Beth Schrader
Tami Wahlin
Ann Pfister
Sue Remes
Jenny Goudreault
Alice Justinak
Sarah Gunhouse
Sara Friedle
Deb Buzar
Marni Tjosaas

Discussion Questions for *The Second*

1) The title of the book, *The Second,* refers to a number of different elements in the story. Which ones are prominent to you?

2) The author uses humor to soften the effects of some serious subjects. Did you find it helpful or distracting?

3) Dr. Malbec's prominence was reduced from earlier drafts. Did you get enough information to form your own conclusions about his character?

4) The author intentionally describes some of the early warning signs and characteristics of mania by weaving them into the story. Can you name any?

5) It takes the physical death of her father to get Colleen to see herself as a grown woman. Is it possible to make that transition while your parents are still alive?

6) Colleen's marriage takes multiple hits in the story. What are some of the reasons their union endures?

7) A six-decade life provides a lot of material to explore. Why do you suppose she chose to share some aspects of her early life in Chapter Two? How do those incidents inform her later life?

8) The doctor-patient relationship figures strongly in the story. Can you relate to any of the good, bad, or indifferent relationships?

9) The stigma of mental illness and mental health care looms large for Colleen. Do you see the impact of stigma changing in society today? Has this book altered the way you view mental illness?

10) The author uses a three-act structure to frame the story. Are the three acts obvious to you? Can you sense when the narrative shifts?

Made in the USA
Monee, IL
07 October 2021